D0603784

Lewis & Clark
COLLEGE

Stephen Dow Beckham

Photography by Robert M. Reynolds

LEWIS & CLARK COLLEGE

CONTENTS

International Standard Book Number 0-9630866-0-X
Library of Congress Number 91-71222
© 1991 by Lewis & Clark College
0615 Southwest Palatine Hill Road • Portland, Oregon 97219 • 503/768-7950
No part of this book may be reproduced
by any means without permission of Lewis & Clark College.
All rights reserved.
Produced by • Graphic Arts Center Publishing Company
P.O. Box 10306 • Portland, Oregon 97210 • 503/226-2402
President • Charles M. Hopkins
Editor-in-Chief • Douglas A. Pfeiffer
Managing Editor • Jean Andrews
Project Manager • Michael Ford, Director of Alumni Relations • Lewis & Clark College
Designers • Robert M. Reynolds and Letha Gibbs Wulf
Separations • Wy'east Color, Inc.
Typographer • Harrison Typesetting, Inc.
Printer • Dynagraphics, Inc.
Bindery • Lincoln & Allen
Sponsor • Lewis & Clark College Alumni Association
Printed in the United States of America

Quotes on pages 9 and 125 © 1987; page 152 © 1990 by Kim R. Stafford
Quotes on page 10 © 1973; pages 61, 69, and 129 © 1977 by William E. Stafford
Quotes on page 52 © 1978; page 63 © 1964 by Vern Rutsala
All quotes used by permission.
Photos on pages 26 and 28 • J. G. Crawford; page 51 • Brubaker Aerial Surveys;
page 73 • Photo Art; page 77 • Lake Oswego Studio; page 78 • Ben Fleischman;
page 84 • Jerome Hart; page 100 • Kyle Cook, '80, and Robert Jenkins, '84;
All other black-and-white photos are from the College archives.

◄ ◄ *Mount Hood stands majestic in the distance
as seen from the Edna Holmes Terrace of the Manor House.*

PRESIDENT'S MESSAGE

Of all human capacities, memory is surely the most trenchant, for it binds us to a past and makes history possible. Perhaps for this reason we personify memory, training it like a willful dog and berating it for its lapses. It "plays tricks" on us, we say, and sometimes it "fails" us.

Memory's products are equally alive. Memories can be keen or dull, vivid or faint. They can tide us over in bad times and hound us when things are otherwise good. Some are too painful to bear; others are our only solace. In all its many guises, memory is wrapped up with our deepest humanity.

Institutions as well as individuals have memories. An institution's memory is continually at work, alive in the rituals it keeps and in the buildings and grounds it maintains. But it is especially alive in the individual memories of all who are or have been a part of it. For this reason an institution chooses not so much to remember as to remember together—to commemorate. It does so especially at the passing of its giants and on the anniversaries of its triumphs.

By a happy turn of fate, 1992 marks three anniversaries for Lewis & Clark College: the 125th year of its founding, the 50th year since its relocation to the Fir Acres estate in Southwest Portland, and the 30th year of its trailblazing efforts in overseas study. A coincidence of this kind calls for celebration; but it is also the occasion for special reflection.

Lewis & Clark College is the fitting response to this double demand—a grateful look back on the way things came to be. As thinkers since Aristotle have recognized, memory and imagination are correlative faculties since each depends on images. The images in this volume are particularly evocative: the finely crafted words of Stephen Dow Beckham and the extraordinary photographs of Robert M. Reynolds.

Those who had a part in the making of the College will find their memories ignited by these images, filled with impressions and episodes that no history, official or otherwise, could capture. Those coming to know the College only through these images will find their imaginations stirred, marvelling at the mettle of forebears who had the courage to dream large dreams and the stamina to make them real. All will be treated to a feast of spirit and to a celebration of the College that is its result.

MICHAEL MOONEY

President
Lewis & Clark College

▲ Herman Brookman, the architect of the Fir Acres estate, placed numerous sculptures of animals on the exterior of the Manor House, including two imperial eagles which mark the entrance.

LIFE OF THE MIND

Nearly one hundred fifty years ago a young American charted a special course in life. Henry Thoreau embarked on a process of self-discovery through observation and reflection. A master of looking at life closely, he later noted why he constructed a cabin and lived for a year at Walden Pond. "I went to the woods because I wished to live deliberately, to front only the essential facts of life, and see if I could not learn what it had to teach, and not, when I came to die, discover that I had not lived." Thoreau sought to wring essence and meaning from life. He touched its fiber, explored its ambiguities, recoiled from its affronts, and drew inspiration from what lay close at hand.

The pursuit of the life of the mind is the noblest of human enterprises. It sets men and women apart from animals and permits the celebration of what it is to be human. It demands imagination and even leaps of faith. Bernard de Fontenelle, an essayist and domineering figure in the French Academy of Sciences, displayed such commitment when in 1658 he published his essays, *A Week's Conversation on the Plurality of Worlds*. Fontenelle permitted himself to raise the intriguing question: is it possible that life exists elsewhere than on earth? The answer was not as important as the speculation. He let go of the blinders and constraints which governed his society to pose a provocative question. Through his essays, he explored pros and cons inherent in the proposition of a plurality of worlds. "I have chosen that Part of Philosophy which is most likely to excite Curiosity," he wrote, "for I think nothing concerns us more than to enquire how this World, which we inhabit, is made; and whether there be any other Worlds like it, which are also inhabited as This is."

These experiences suggest exercise of the will of the individual. That will, while influenced and even nurtured from without, ultimately must come from within. Some catch it; others dodge it; a few miss it altogether. John Tucker Scott, an Oregon-bound emigrant in 1852, dangled before his children the opportunity to grow through new experiences. He urged his teenagers to keep a collective diary of their travels. When their interest waned or they were too tired to write, he took over, but penned only a few lines before one daughter, Abigail, again began writing. In spite of chores and tending a dying mother and later a much-loved little brother, Abigail Scott responded well to her father's challenge. During her journey across the American West, she realized the importance of sharp observation. She turned her Oregon Trail adventure into a course in watching, writing, and reflecting.

She learned the value of discipline and practice, and mastered the exercise of the will. As a young wife, Abigail Scott Duniway crafted one of Oregon's first novels, *Captain Gray's Company* (1859). The book drew heavily on her diary and exhibited her commitment to study and to causes. Duniway rose above adversity, poverty, and family responsibility. She became a public speaker, then a newspaper editor and publisher, a poet and essayist, and—ultimately—a national figure in the women's suffrage movement. Life was her college; discipline, her mentor. Commitment inspired her cause.

◄ *Carved face on the Manor, by Roi Morin.* ▲ *A 1757 copy of* A Week's Conversation on the Plurality of Worlds, *by Bernard de Fontenelle.*

Practice is essential. Musicians grow by playing scales, programming fingering, memorizing scores, and probing for the composer's meaning. Runners strengthen muscles and lungs, master the pace, and focus upon critically timed bursts of energy. Artists coordinate the eye and hand to craft what is imagined. Potters' wheels turn, and turn again, as clay takes shape. Philosophers reflect, argue, and lay out sequential arguments, realizing that proof demands rigor, review, and revision. Scientists posit hypotheses, assemble apparatus, mount experiments, observe what happens, and draw conclusions. All these labors are founded on practice and are part of nurturing reason. For some, these become "habits of the heart."

A wise man said: "give me a lever long enough and a place to stand, and I can turn the world." College is both lever and standing place, for it exists to celebrate the life of the mind. Plato's Academy, medieval universities, seminaries, "independent academies," land grant universities, and private colleges have all helped craft levers long enough. They have drawn upon resources, abilities, teachers, and the purposeful grooming of students to help turn the world.

For more than two centuries American colleges had focused on spiritual training. Christians demanded a literate pastorate. In denominational schools they trained lay and clerical leaders and believers through Bible-based curriculum and sectarian practice. In time, some institutions slipped from churchly control. Sometimes the mission commitment changed; Christian education no longer drew benevolence and schools grew increasingly secular.

Whatever the educational enterprise, those that have succeeded demanded the best. What is best? A commitment to excellence is at the heart of achievement. The trick is to reach farther than the grasp, to extend the hand, to widen the embrace and to do so with rigor. The commitment to excellence comes from within. It flows from leaders, teachers, and students who thirst for knowledge.

John Howard, president of Lewis & Clark College for more than two decades, delivered his charge to graduating classes. "You came as empty vessels," he said, implying that four years of study handily filled the containers. For many alumni, this was correct. College became a pivotal moment of filling, extending, testing, probing, and seeking. It was where students learned to draw on inner strength and muster the discipline to try harder, to try again, to achieve.

Those who embrace the life of the mind are always students. This is as true of the teacher as of the first-term freshman. College is where faculty and students are engaged in discovery as learners. Sometimes discovery taps latent talents; other times it nurtures those already known. Sometimes college is the process of daring to imagine what might be. It is a place of encounter with people, ideas, orthodoxy, and heresy. At its best, college becomes a bit like Thoreau's year at Walden Pond. It is a schooling where those who embrace its full measure ultimately say: "I have lived."

Alfred, Lord Tennyson wrestled with the meaning of human existence. In the poem, "Ulysses," he drew inspiration from the *Odyssey*, by Homer, and from life's experiences. Tennyson later commented that crafting the poem gave him "the feeling about the need of going forward and braving the struggle of life." He wrote:

Though much is taken, much abides; and though
We are not now that strength which in old days
Moved earth and heaven; that which we are, we are;
One equal temper of heroic hearts,
Made weak by time and fate, but strong in will
To strive, to seek, and not to yield.

▲ College Outdoor trip participants hike across the Alvord Desert of southeastern Oregon. ► The terraced water features of the Fir Acres estate include a sculpture fountain, a waterfall, the reflection pond, the Gorgon fountain, a fish pond, and a swimming pool.

*Solitude is the scientific method
of the human spirit.*

KIM R. STAFFORD
"A Walk in Early May," *Having Everything Right,* 1987

The whole day is your gift:
hold it and read a leaf at a time,
never hurried, never waiting.

PROFESSOR WILLIAM E. STAFFORD
"Some Days of Its Gift," *Someday, Maybe*, 1973

Those magic words – "To strive, to seek, and not to yield" – are at the heart of living purposefully, intently, and with self-awareness. "The truth shall set you free" is engraved above many library entry doors. To find truth demands striving and seeking. That is a worthy exploration and is at the heart of what college is all about. Some make the pursuit corporately and comfortably in large classes; others, like Thoreau, thrive best in programs of independent study. Some share their moments of inspiration, like Fontenelle, with a larger world. Others store up their insights, hoarding them as their own personal treasure. And some with a philanthropic bent share their talents and lives generously, like Abigail Scott Duniway, so that others may find a better, more equitable world for their having been part of it.

In his inaugural remarks in 1990, Michael Joseph Mooney articulated a clear vision for Lewis & Clark College as it moved toward a new century:

> [A college] *is not . . . a home, but neither is it a mere massing of individuals. Students come here for a curriculum that faculty set, and to do it in ways that we believe will form them best as persons and as citizens. Like every curriculum, that of this college aims to emancipate our students through knowledge. But it aims at a great deal more as well: in the way it is organized, in the forms of pedagogy it employs, in the cocurricular activities it engenders, and in the use of resources it implies, it seeks to join our students to their experiences in four very precise ways, to engender in them four very definite habits of the heart. And in these habits, I believe, we have our character as a college.*

President Mooney affirmed that college should build a "sense of the present," "the passion for inquiry," "the habit of environmental respect," and "the engagement with other cultures." In these a college helps mold the character of its students and helps them understand and shape the communities in which they will live.

College years are moments of discovery. They involve finding self, others, ideas, and passions. They school students in how to channel and govern their abilities. "From exertion come wisdom and purity," extolled an American writer, and "from sloth ignorance and sensuality." The pursuit of learning demands exertion and holds the promise of wisdom, if not purity. Sloth may feed ignorance, if not sensuality. So the ethic of practice, the discipline of attending to details, and the quest for excellence in all things hold the greatest promises. These are essential ingredients in the pursuit of the life of the mind.

College is also memory, the sum of things done, not done, times good and bad, of growth and responsibility. College is something held individually and collectively. It is the sum of a person's thoughts and feelings. It is the sum of friendships, moments of shared joy, and frustration. It is a record of tests passed, things failed, realizations of work not quite complete, and times of spectacular accomplishment. College becomes something carried away, closely held, occasionally celebrated, and a passage indelibly marking each participant.

College is a realization, a time of maturing, spreading wings, building new ties, and defining life's labors. It is a process of reaching potential, daring to extend the self, and probing for what might be. It is a time of testing character and values. It is a time of discovering that learning is lifelong, not just a few years. College is a realization that the life of the mind is the noblest of human enterprises. It is the time of discovering how to live and how to live deliberately.

◄ Inscribed in the library – built in 1967 and named for Aubrey R. Watzek – John Ruskin's words speak eloquently: "When we build, let us think we build forever. Let it not be for present delight, nor for present use alone: let it be such work as our descendants will thank us for. . . ." ▲ Professor Bill Hunt reviews an orchestral score.

◄ Violinist Jae-Kyung Kim, '91. ▼ The Albany Quadrangle walls demonstrate a patina, which has been enhanced not only by the passing of time but also by the abundant rainfall in Oregon.

▼ The outdoor swimming pool, which was completed in 1925, features the commissioned metalwork of Oscar Bach. ► The College Outdoor program rafting trip on the Deschutes River.

*Allow me enough poetic license
to assert that no faculty member —
at Lewis and Clark or elsewhere —
is ever satisfied.*

DEAN OF FACULTY LEWIS THAYER
Commencement Address, 1969

◄ The "King of Bali," composed and directed by music professor Vincent McDermott, combined theatre and music of Western and Eastern cultures. The opera, featuring the College's "Venerable Showers of Beauty" Indonesian gamelan, premiered at Fir Acres Theatre in 1989 and returned for encore performances in 1990.
▲ Professor of Psychology Helena Carlson confers with students.

We send you forth with love and respect.
We ask you to serve your soul, your society,
and your destiny nobly and well.
Leave the world better than you found it.
You have the capacity to do so.

PRESIDENT JOHN R. HOWARD
Charge to the Class of 1969

▲ President Michael Mooney welcomes the class of 1991. Left to right: Susan Resneck Parr, vice president, dean of College; Rabbi Emanuel Rose, chair, Board of Trustees; Mooney; Ambassador David Miller, Jr., commencement speaker; Becky Johnson, trustee; David Taylor, '74, president, Alumni Association. Student marshals are Pidge Pelletreau, '92, ASLC president; and Joseph Martorano, '92, ASLC student academic affairs vice president. Signing for the hearing impaired is Karen Jill Bailey '87, M.Ed. ▶ The mace, an Indian symbol of authority, leads commencement processions.

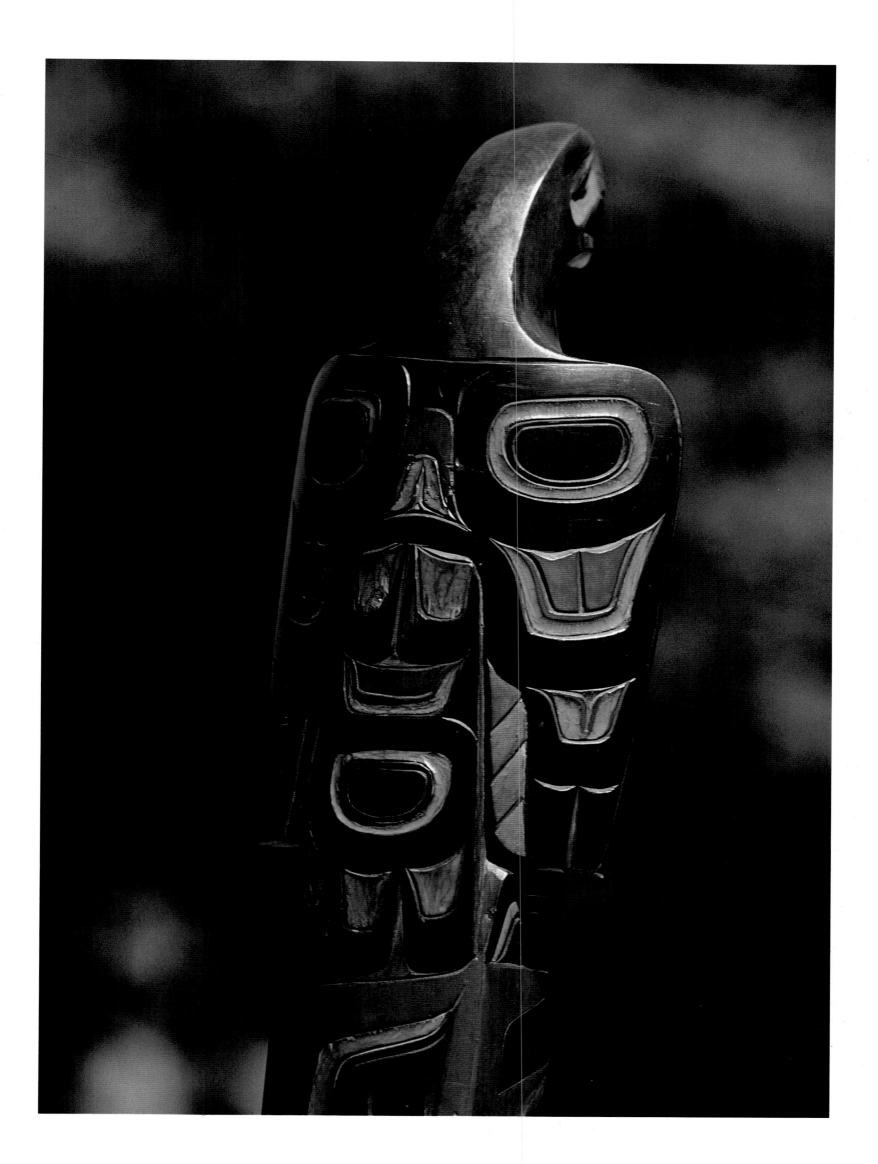

◄ Agnes Flanagan Chapel and vaulter at the Eldon Fix Track.
▼ Housed in the Aubrey Watzek Library Heritage Room are special collections of Western Americana and fine printing. Among the College's treasured volumes are the Lewis & Clark Expedition Collection of Drs. Eldon G. and Robert Chuinard, the library of John and LaRae Caughey on California and the Southwest, and the collections of Francis Haines, Sr., on the Columbia Plateau.

ALBANY COLLEGE AND
NORTHWESTERN COLLEGE OF LAW

The world of the nineteenth-century emigrants to the Oregon country underwent dramatic change as they left the eastern woodlands to traverse the plains and mountains of North America. Their reports quickened the imaginations of thousands who made the decision to go West. In Oregon they began anew to erect shelter, find gainful employment, wrest a living from the land, and craft institutions to weave together the social fabric of their new world. Momentarily they held within their grasp the opportunity to strike out boldly and create a new order in society, the economy, education, and religious practices and organization. Instead, as creatures of habit, they labored willfully to reconstruct, as rapidly as possible, everything they knew from someplace else. Tugging at their hearts and lives were old ways of doing things. They had carried not only supplies to sustain life on the Oregon Trail; they brought a heavy load of intellectual baggage to furnish a world on the same terms as in their former homes.

Oregon's frontier settlers established courts, churches, schools, villages, and social organizations to govern and bond their communities. They sought to replicate the classical or Greek Revival buildings of the Mississippi Valley on their Oregon farms or in their new towns. They carried their prejudice, sectarian difference, and bigotry to their new land just as they brought their talent, energy, and determination. Habit dictated their ways; innovation had little place.

"The object of your mission is to explore the Missouri river, & such principal stream of it as, by it's course & communication with the waters of the Pacific Ocean, may offer the most direct & practicable communication across this continent, for the purposes of commerce." In these instructions in 1803 to Meriwether Lewis, President Thomas Jefferson laid the foundation for drawing the Oregon country into the national design of the United States. Lewis turned to his army companion, William Clark, to share in carrying out Jefferson's grand plan. The Lewis and Clark Expedition fired imaginations and fostered the idea that, in time, the nation would span the continent. Jefferson envisioned an expedition founded on utility but couched in the discovery of information. Not only were Lewis and Clark to seek a route of water transportation, they were to collect, observe, record, and assess the resources of the lands they traversed. They were to secure useful knowledge to help their contemporaries and future generations.

The Oregon country gained good press. Nicholas Biddle's two-volume edition of the *Journals of Lewis and Clark* (1814) proved so popular it was literally read to pieces. The explorers' narratives confirmed their success in meeting Jefferson's assignment and told of the great forests, bountiful runs of fish, and Indians. Washington Irving's *Astoria* (1836) and *Adventures of Captain Bonneville* (1837) recounted the labors of fur seekers and profits of trading enterprises in the watershed of the Columbia River. Coupled with these accounts was the buoyant enthusiasm of publicists like Hall Jackson Kelley who touted Oregon's possibilities for emigrants.

By the 1830s the Second Great Awakening had quickened a national commitment to missions and led to concern about the souls

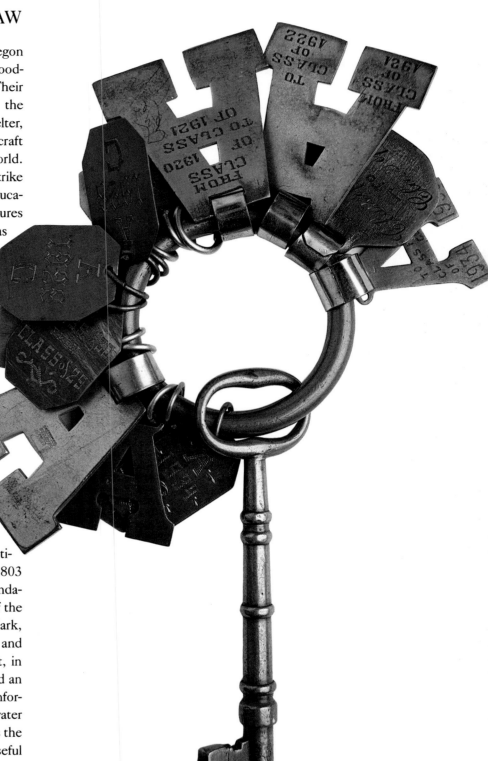

◄ *First graduates, 1873, were Maria Irvine, Cora Irvine, Weltha Young, and Mary Hannon.* ▲ *Albany senior class key ring, 1917-38.*

of Pacific Northwest Indians. In 1834 Rev. Jason Lee emigrated to Oregon to establish Methodist missions in the Willamette Valley. Two years later the Whitmans and Spaldings, sponsored by the American Board of Commissioners for Foreign Missions, settled on the Columbia Plateau. The ABCFM was an ecumenical effort, a sharing of mission dollars of Presbyterians, Congregationalists, and Dutch Reformed churches. In 1839 Catholic priests descended the Columbia River from Canada to perform marriages, baptize the children of Hudson's Bay Company *voyageurs,* and build missions. The missionaries confirmed what fur seekers already knew: the Pacific Northwest had great potential. It was amenable for farming, stock raising, and production of commodities such as fruits, berries, and cereal crops. When the scientific reports of Charles Wilkes and John Fremont, who visited Oregon in 1841 and 1843, confirmed these realities, a nation stood ready to turn west.

Currents of restlessness and westward yearning ran deep. Even transcendentalist Henry Thoreau caught the fever. "Let me live where I will, on this side is the city, on that the wilderness, and ever I am leaving the city more and more, and withdrawing into the wilderness," he wrote. "I should not lay so much stress on this fact, if I did not believe that something like this is the prevailing tendency of my countrymen. I must walk toward Oregon, and not toward Europe." Tens of thousands of Americans found themselves of like mind in the 1840s. For two generations their families had pressed beyond the Appalachians and Alleghenies into the valleys of the Ohio and Mississippi until Euramerican settlement stood at the end of the vast, tractless prairies of the continent's heartland. Uncertainty prevailed about life in such a place, but Oregon was another consideration. Its forested hills, healthful climate, fertile valleys, abundant waterpower, rivers and harbors, and land—seemingly for the taking—possessed irresistible magnetism.

Prophetic voices urged them onward. "The trade of the Pacific Ocean, of the western coast of North America, and of Eastern Asia," thundered Sen. Thomas Benton, "will all take its track; and not only for ourselves but for our posterity." Benton laid out his image of a great "Passage to India" that would tie Atlantic to Pacific. "An American road to India through the heart of our country," he asserted, "will revive upon its line all the wonders of which we have read—and eclipse them. The western wilderness, from the Pacific to the Mississippi, will start into life under its touch."

At heart many American frontier settlers were land speculators. They hungered to sell out for a profit, take up a new claim, labor on improvements, and then repeat the process. During the 1840s when Senators Benton and Lewis Linn introduced bills in Congress offering up to one thousand acres free to each settler who went to Oregon, the stage was set for massive emigration. Starting as a trickle in 1841, it swelled to more than nine hundred people in 1843 and grew to more than three thousand in 1845.

Those who set out for the West were either men and women of capital or young people fired by adventure and the prospect of finding their fortunes in a new land. Overland emigration required a wagon, teams, harnesses, tools, clothing, weaponry, trading goods, and food supplies for a journey of four to six months. A few hundred dollars in gold or silver were also a good idea because emergency supplies, replacement livestock, or repairs at the forts scattered along the Oregon Trail were costly and sometimes necessary.

Thomas and Walter Monteith were among the ten thousand who came to Oregon in that decade. In 1847 the brothers outfitted wagons and ox teams and traveled overland. The following year they

purchased a provisional land claim for $400 along the Willamette River near its confluence with Calapooia Creek, surveyed sixty acres which they platted into lots, and—after a brief sojourn in California's gold mines—began promotion of Albany, Oregon. They named the community for the capital of New York, their home state. The Monteiths brought capital, vision, and energy to a new land. They translated their aspirations into action and, possessing a bit of luck as well as perseverance, succeeded. They erected a Greek Revival residence facing the river in 1849, opened a mercantile store the next year, and—in time—built the Magnolia City Mills and Albany City Mills. The wheels of their industry transformed wheat to flour, and harvests into salable commodities for transit down the Willamette to the Asian market.

In their businesslike way the Monteith brothers in Linn County carried to fruition not only the dreams of commerce of Jefferson and Benton but the poetic vision of Walt Whitman:

I chant the world on my Western Sea; . . .
I chant the new empire, grander than any before—
 As in a vision it comes to me;
I chant America, the Mistress—I chant a greater supremacy;
I chant, projected, a thousand blooming cities yet, in time,
 on those groups of sea-islands; . . .
I chant commerce opening, the sleep of ages having done
 its work—races, reborn, refresh'd . . . .

The missing ingredient in the community along the Willamette River was a college. As town developers near the western sea, the Monteiths were prepared to be generous.

A spirit of education coursed through American life. Ideals of an articulate electorate who could read, write, and think suggested the need to nurture young minds to fit them for responsibilities of citizenship. To read the Bible, explore the meaning of scriptures, and bring succeeding generations to the faith required schooling. To cipher and calculate profit and loss, enter business agreements, and engage in commerce demanded other skills. By the 1800s, people realized that education was basic to their way of life. It became of national importance to develop an educated citizenry.

Oregon's efforts began modestly. In 1848, Henry Spalding, a Presbyterian missionary who had fled the Nez Perce Indians during the Cayuse War the previous year, opened a private school in a log cabin near Brownsville in the mid-Willamette Valley. Others organized subscription schools where parents paid a teacher to work with students for a few months. Linn County and Albany, its seat of government, mirrored this development. Between 1852, when the public school movement commenced, and 1854, when limited tax funding became more certain, residents developed twenty-four school districts. Three years later the school boards adopted a course of study: *Webster's Speller, Davies' Arithmetic, Olney's Geography, Kirkham's Grammar,* and the *Student's Reader.*

Across western Oregon, however, church leaders aspired for schools with greater rigor, advanced studies, and preparation of lay and clerical leaders for the ministry. Rev. Edward R. Geary, a Presbyterian minister who came with his wife by sea in 1851, knew the value of such education. He had attended Jefferson College and Western Theological Seminary; his wife was a graduate of Mount Holyoke Seminary. Geary and others secured a charter from the territorial legislature in 1854 for Union Point Academy. He served as

Albany and Linn County have been "dry" since
1906 and we believe that the licensed saloon will
never return to the county.
To the south and west the contiguous counties are
without saloons, and as
our own county reaches the mountains there is
danger from but one side.

Albany College *Bulletin,* 1909

▲ Erected on land that was donated by the Monteith family, this
original wood-frame building served the College from 1867 until the
move to the "Monteith Campus" in 1925. The architecture of the
building reflected the vernacular of the Oregon frontier: Italianate
brackets, a cupola with Gothic window, and Greek revival pilasters.

▲ The tableau, "Battle of the Amazons," was one of several popular productions in the 1890s under the direction of the professor of rhetoric and elocution. Taught according to the principles of Delsarte, this physical training program included pantomime, theatre, and gymnastics, designed to promote a sense of harmony.

its first president, but, when he became Superintendent of Indian Affairs, the school languished; it closed in 1859.

Residents of Albany continued to hope for a Presbyterian school. In 1866 they planned a strategy to draw on the assets of the defunct Union Point Academy and the Monteith brothers' offer of a school site. They launched fund-raising efforts to secure cash and promises for $8,000. On that foundation they built a two-story wood-frame building to house the Albany Collegiate Institute. On February 2, 1867, they secured a charter from the state legislature and in October were ready to offer courses "with the view of increasing knowledge in the liberal arts and sciences for the development of character under moral and religious influences."

Albany's "college" possessed no specific distinction. Methodists launched Willamette University in Salem; Congregationalists supported Pacific University in Forest Grove; Baptists had McMinnville College in McMinnville; and the Church of the Brethren founded Philomath College in Benton County. Other church-related schools either preceded or followed the venture in Albany. Nearby was the Methodists' Santiam Academy in Lebanon and the Cumberland Presbyterians' Mineral Springs College at Sodaville—both Linn County schools vying for students and Christian benevolence with Albany Collegiate Institute. In fact, residents of Albany erected a public school in 1855, expanded it to four rooms in 1880, and by 1889-90 rebuilt it as Central School with ten rooms and 364 students. To survive, Albany Collegiate Institute had to offer something special, secure endowments, draw strong administrators and teachers, and find stability. The institution struggled with each.

Rev. William Monteith, brother of Albany's developers, was appointed the first president. His tenure of one year set a pattern in administration. In 1867 forty students enrolled. Most were in the "graded" and "preparatory" divisions, for the school took students from elementary grades through college. Beyond the new building, the greatest asset was books from the Albany Library and Literary Institute which turned over its property to the College. Sigma Phi, the men's literary society, served as custodian of the library.

The school's commitment to maintain "wholesome restraints" on the students and to provide equality of experience for men and women and boys and girls worked to Albany's advantage. "The daily association of young ladies and gentlemen, in the presence of their teachers, exerts a most salutary effect upon the *manners of both*," said the administration. This coeducational setting tended "powerfully to render the young men courteous, self-respectful, refined and manly, and the young women modest, decorous, graceful and womanly." The promise of compliant, submissive, well-behaved children persuaded parents in 1869-70 to enroll eighty-six students.

The curriculum focused on the classics and traditional courses. After assuring prospective students in 1878 that the College hall's "ventilation is ample for health and comfort," the catalog laid out four terms of work from September to June. The catalog was mute about the primary department which enrolled most of the students. In the first year of "preparatory" study, students received instruction in grammar, arithmetic, composition, astronomy, U.S. history, and Latin. The second year continued Latin, with special work on the writings of Julius Caesar, introductory Greek, algebra, geography, and natural philosophy. "Advanced branches cannot *in any case* be pursued until those which are preparatory have been *mastered*," warned the catalog. Fees ran from five dollars in the primary division to twelve dollars per term for collegiate students. There were extra fees for music, drawing, painting, French, and German.

"Energy and Thorough Work is the Motto of Our School" asserted professors and trustees. The offerings by 1878-79 confirmed that purpose. Freshmen studied American history, algebra, physiology, Virgil, Cicero, and Homer. Sophomores coped with Herodotus, Horace, Tacitus, trigonometry, geology, zoology, and "Memorabilia." Third-year students read Livy, and studied botany, mechanics, French or German grammar, "American Geometry," and calculus. Seniors took mathematical astronomy, psychology, political economy, and moral science and read Racine or Goethe.

Students pursuing the scientific degree were permitted to skip Greek and reduce their work in Latin. Those in the classical track had to take prescribed courses in Greek and Latin. Students seeking a "normal" education to become teachers earned a certificate for completion of a two-year program but did not receive degrees. The only deviation of programs among the genders was that "young ladies will be allowed to substitute other branches for the higher mathematics." Those "other branches" were modern languages.

In the 1880s the College prescribed its programs for advanced students with more precision. Those in the "classical" course faced Xenophon's *Anabasis*, Homer's *Iliad*, "except the catalogue of the ships," and thirty exercises in Greek composition. Students in the "scientific" course coped with Sallust's *Jugurtha*, Virgil's *Aeneid*, Cicero's *Orations*, surveying, navigation, "Conic Sections," calculus, and "Evidences of Natural and Revealed Religion." The College imposed written midterm and final exams throughout the four terms in all branches of study. The elementary program consisted of four grades. Entering students had to sight-read from the *Second Reader* and recite the multiplication tables through six-times.

The substantial curriculum belied the instability of the institution. Part of the problem lay in the agreement reached in 1868. The Board of Trustees turned over the College to the president, who received tuition, determined salaries, paid bills, and ran the school. The board maintained the Presbyterian connection, addressed the institution's moral tone and character, but kept its distance. Some presidents proved good managers; others got into difficulty: faculty rebellions, student discipline, and perennial deficits. The Albany location—though served by steamboats and, after 1872, by the Oregon & California Railroad—failed to draw students from other areas. Competition also hurt, for the state established the University of Oregon in 1876 in Eugene and in 1886 took over a struggling Methodist college in nearby Corvallis as a land-grant university. These competitors and their proximity checked the growth and threatened the stability of the Albany Collegiate Institute.

Part of the problem also lay in its strict rules. Young people in the late nineteenth century wanted to dance, roller skate, swim, and ride bicycles. The College, however, focused on the obligatory "literary societies" and religious services under faculty control. The Erodelphians for women and the Albany College Literary Society (ACLS) for men offered "drill of select speaking, essay writing, debate, criticism, extemporare speaking, and the forms of parliamentary usage" for all over age fourteen. Unlike state schools, all pupils at Albany had to have a Bible, song book, dictionary, and—by 1885—*Monteith's Comprehensive Geography*. They attended daily chapel but on Sundays might worship at the church of their choice. Some enrolled because of these offerings; others went elsewhere.

The inability of the collegiate division to attract more than a hundred students for the institution's first fifty-five years was thus a result of several factors. While Albany College recruited talented and well-trained faculty, including a number from Princeton and

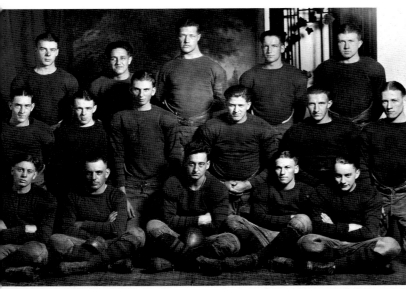

▲ In 1903 the Albany football team defeated Oregon Agricultural College (later OSU), 6-0. From 1931-35, the team lost a record 28 consecutive games. Organized in 1899, the women's basketball team was coached by John Tait and Rev. Curtis Stevenson, Albany United Presbyterian Church. In 1905 the team won state championship, defeating Oregon Agricultural College (OSU), 20-12. The 1896 Albany Collegiate Institute-Community Band, directed by Professor Charles Howland, involved a brass section and one dog.

other Presbyterian-related schools, it struggled. The 1887 catalog spoke of the strong curriculum but lamented that the "gymnasium is only a temporary one annexed to the building." It described the cupola atop the College and its view, but observed: "the College has no apparatus for practical work in astronomy." It described the library's "embryonic state" and the institution's eagerness to receive "any curiosities and specimens" for its mineralogical cabinet, a collection borrowed from a resident of Portland. The required course in physiology, it noted, had been "materially assisted" by Dr. G. W. Maston, who had loaned his microscope to the College.

The College espoused high standards but suffered from limited resources. Presidents and faculty came and went. At times closure seemed certain. Repeatedly, survival depended on the nurturing of the town's residents and the sense of mission and pride of the presbytery in its only viable Oregon college. The College also had special friends, including Rev. Samuel Irvine of the Albany United Presbyterian Church and his children and grandchildren who attended the school, and William S. Ladd and Henry Corbett. In 1883 these two businessmen pledged a total of $10,000 for an endowment, provided it was triple matched within three years. In spite of concerted efforts which cost two presidents their jobs, the College was unable to secure the match.

The enrollment growth to nearly one hundred students in 1892 and the nearby ten-room Central School in Albany convinced school officials to enlarge the College building. The decision proved nearly fatal, for though it led to substantial two-story wings on the original structure, it saddled the school with a debt which coincided with the Panic of 1893. The only choice was a mortgage at 10 percent interest. William M. Ladd and Henry Corbett rescued the school in 1896 by paying the overdue interest to get the College out of court. In 1900 the combined energies of President Wallace Howe Lee, Dr. Edgar Hill of the First Presbyterian Church in Portland, and residents of Albany finally freed the College of debt.

For the next thirty years Albany College tried to strengthen its curriculum, faculty, and finances. It brought its offerings into line with state guidelines, especially in teacher preparation courses. Under Presidents Lee and Crooks it gained administrative stability: each served a decade. The enrollment mirrored College division progress: nineteen students in 1895, thirty-four in 1904, and more than one hundred in 1925. In 1901 Lee purchased the Orphan's Home building and moved it to campus to become Tremont Hall, a women's dormitory. In 1905 the trustees officially adopted the name Albany College, assumed fiscal responsibility for the institution and negotiations with faculty, transferred ownership to the Synod of Oregon, and established the bachelor of arts degree.

These changes and a shift from the nineteenth-century classical curriculum were long overdue. Albany College faced competition from the rapid proliferation of public high schools as well as the growth of state institutions with far greater resources. The trustees authorized a capital campaign in 1906. It lurched forward, stopped, succeeded in Albany, failed in Portland, then took on new life when East Coast donors responded to President Crooks and reached toward $100,000. In 1911 James Hill, railroad magnate and owner of the Oregon Electric, which passed through Albany, pledged $50,000 toward an endowment of $250,000. These developments drew capital both from Portland donors and statewide.

Looking to the future, the College in 1913 acquired forty-six acres on the edge of town for a new campus. This provoked Monteith heirs to file suit to regain the original campus. They lost in

▲ The early curriculum focused on the classics, though student life centered on obligatory literary societies, faculty-controlled religious services, sports, and music. High standards were required for students and faculty alike, and limited resources were the norm.

Dr. Lee [Wallace Howe Lee] *expressed desire that*
disturbances in chapel
be muffled. Also sets forth principles
that chapel was not place for spooning.

Orange Peal, 1917

▲ "Remember always to express all you feel – in service – looking toward a more truly Christian world." – Professor Fred G. Bale. Scrapbook courtesy L. Annette Adcock, '29. ▶ Professor emeritus William N. Shearer, Albany College, '31, participated in President Michael Mooney's inauguration in 1990. Shearer taught chemistry at Albany and Lewis & Clark until he retired in 1977. He was sports historian for the Pioneer Athletic Hall of Fame Selection Committee and was elected to the Hall in 1987. Over twenty-five members of the Shearer-Shibley family have attended the College.

the Oregon Supreme Court. The expansion of the library to more than five thousand volumes and hopes for a better future led in 1915 to an accrediting visit by the U.S. Bureau of Education. Its endorsement and recommendations sealed the fate of the preparatory division and led to efforts to shorten teacher contact hours and improve resources. In 1916 the College announced that the Hill gift, fully matched, had helped create an endowment of $250,000, yet the funds seemed beyond reach. Hill created a complex formula for endowment management. The new funds held out the prospect of better times but did not help meet day-to-day expenses.

In 1916 Pacific University in Forest Grove launched an ambitious merger idea which captured the interest and commitment of many trustees except those from Linn County. Tension gripped the board, enrollment skidded—especially as young men enlisted to serve in World War I—the presbytery struggled with what to do, and Hill's endowment formula worked inexorably on. The turn of events at Albany seemed to echo in the lines of "Gerontion" by T. S. Eliot:

Think now
History has many cunning passages, contrived corridors
And issues, deceives with whispering ambitions,
Guides us by vanities. Think now
She gives when our attention is distracted
And what she gives, gives with such supple confusions
That the giving famishes the craving.

In 1920 Rev. A. M. Williams, a graduate of 1896 and the new College president, proposed a solution to the "supple confusions," a situation grown more ominous by loss of accreditation. Albany College would embrace Self-Help. All students would work, the presbytery would assume greater control, and construction would begin on three buildings on the new "Monteith Campus" on the edge of town. Dr. Clarence Wilson Greene, who became president in 1923, embraced the idea, envisioning twenty acres for buildings, fifteen acres for "self-help industries," and the remaining property devoted to a college farm and dairy. The bequest of Caroline Kamm of Portland enabled the College to erect William H. Gray Hall in 1925. The next year the College moved Tremont Hall to the new campus, refaced it with brick, and named it Woodward Hall.

By 1929 the College realized the Self-Help formula was more burden than bounty. In spite of all efforts neither community nor College found industrial jobs for students. The College abandoned Self-Help and again sought national support. A bequest of $100,000 by Eric Hauser in 1930 seemed to herald better times and enabled the College to erect Hauser Gymnasium, which seated six hundred. In 1931 Albany College secured accreditation by the Northwest Association of Secondary and Higher Schools, gained membership in the Association of American Colleges, and obtained tentative admittance to the Pacific Northwest Intercollegiate Athletic Conference. Each step forward, however, seemed checked by looming fiscal disaster and the Great Depression.

Albany College was not alone in the dire times of the 1930s. Individuals, families, businesses, local governments all teetered on the edge. The benevolence of Albany residents, the Presbyterian church, support of trustees, and labors of the Women's Albany College League contributed to survival. The faculty took notes, accepted pay cuts of up to forty percent, or even endured no salary at all. Alice Graham, College librarian, continued her duties solely for a room in the dormitory and meals in the student commons.

C. W. Platt, a Portland attorney, accountant, and trustee, sensed by 1932 that financial affairs were out of control. Platt drew in new trustees, renegotiated the mortgage, and staved off foreclosure by bondholders. During the 1933-34 school year a few faculty and trustees realized that in more than seventy years the College had grown but little, yet in Portland resided a large population. A few Presbyterian leaders agreed. Over the opposition of the president of the Board of Trustees, some Albany trustees, and several faculty members, the board decided on June 5, 1934, to offer courses in Portland for fall term. Four years later the last class graduated from the Albany campus. A new future beckoned but its course lay many miles north of where the Monteith brothers sought their fortunes.

"One must be drenched in words, literally soaked in them, to have the right ones form themselves into the proper pattern at the right moment," observed Hart Crane. The crafting of words in careful cadence, sequential argument and prescription is at the heart of the legal profession. Custodians of law must think logically, speak persuasively, and write clearly. Their profession demands discipline, research, reflection, review, and performance. These skills are ones of mastery, practice, and study. Oregon's need for lawyers grew as her economy matured and complex interactions developed among corporations, partners, and individuals. Where once "reading law" with a practitioner had sufficed, by the 1880s society demanded formal training and certification of competency in the profession. Northwestern College of Law, founded in 1884 in Portland by Richard Hopwood Thornton, responded to those needs.

Thornton devoted his life to words and the law. Born in England in 1845, he emigrated to Canada and then to the United States. He began formal study of law in Washington, D. C., and graduated in 1878 from Georgetown University's law school. Three years later, Thornton launched a study of Americanisms. Words and their usage consumed his spare time and ultimately led to his two-volume work, *An American Glossary*, published in London. Teaching law and working with its principles increasingly appealed to the scholarly Thornton, as he tired of the repetition of daily work.

Possibly through a former classmate at Georgetown, Thornton learned of opportunities in Oregon. In 1883 he wrote to federal Judge Matthew Paul Deady: "I wish to offer my services to some institution of learning as Junior Lecturer in a Law School." He explained that he had prepared a course in Common Law and was proceeding with others on "Evidence," "Equity," and "Negotiable Paper." "I am confident it can be made useful," he wrote. The state then had no formal program for legal education; however, Deady, chair of the Board of Regents of the University of Oregon, showed interest. Thornton kept corresponding. When Deady brought the proposal for law instruction to the board late that year, the members rejected it. The uncertainty of enrollment and Thornton's request for a salary guarantee of $1,000 were determining factors.

Over the next few months, Thornton persisted. "I am accustomed to careful work . . . I think the board will be satisfied of my fitness for the post, on seeing what I have done," he concluded. Deady invited Thornton to Portland, and, in June 1884, the two met with the Board of Regents in Eugene. Deady's diary summed up succinctly the results of the interview: "Established a School of Law at Portland and elected Mr. Richard H. Thornton, Professor." As was the case with Albany College, the governing body assumed no financial responsibility. Thornton was to charge what he could, manage as well as possible, and keep any profits.

*I can visualize development
of a Presbyterian sponsored college
in Portland which will become
one of the major institutions of the West.*

PRESIDENT THOMAS BIBB

Report on Albany College to Oregon Presbyteries, 1938

▲ In 1938, Albany College opened its doors in space leased from Temple Beth Israel at Southwest 13th and Main in Portland. The school was without a president or academic accreditation.

▲ The imprint of the environment of western Oregon is evident in the marriage of structure and function in the faculty law library, in the Swindells Legal Research Center. More than twenty-five full-time faculty are complemented by adjunct practitioners and jurists from Portland to teach nearly seven hundred students in day and evening divisions. Librarian Peter Nycum shown in photo.

For the next eighteen years Thornton ran the University of Oregon School of Law. He made law study accessible by charging low tuition and offering night courses. Judge Deady, former Oregon Supreme Court justices Erasmus Shattuck and Lewis McArthur, and prominent Portland attorneys taught in the school. Thornton coped with neglect by the University, criticism from the Oregon Bar Association, and a self-admitted prickly personality. Under doctor's orders in 1903, he left the institution and in 1905 resigned as dean. Belatedly, in 1923 the University of Oregon acknowledged his singular contributions and awarded him an honorary doctorate.

Judge Calvin Gantenbein became the second dean and in 1906 presided over curriculum expansion to three years of study. In 1913 the Board of Regents decided to move the law program to Eugene; neither faculty nor students agreed. In 1915 Gantenbein resigned from the University of Oregon, purchased the library and assets of the Portland facility, retained virtually all students and staff (except the registrar), and taught under the name, Northwestern College of Law. When World War I depleted staff and enrollment, Gantenbein assumed multiple responsibilities. In 1919 District Court Judge J. Hunt Hendrickson became the third dean. Hendrickson introduced the casebook method and a fourth-year program.

Over the years Northwestern College of Law continued to draw on the substantial legal talent of Portland to teach its students. Federal judges, state justices, and practicing attorneys taught in the College–some for decades. The College survived the Depression only to face imminent closure in 1943 when enrollment dropped to sixteen because of World War II. Judge John Gantenbein, son of the second dean, sold his home and borrowed money to keep the College alive. While he served in the war, his wife, Alice, ran the school along with Robert Miller, who was acting dean. Judge James Crawford became the fourth dean as enrollments swelled. Dorothy Cornelius joined the staff in 1956 as secretary and registrar; she was the first full-time employee. In 1958 Judge Gantenbein turned over control to a non-profit corporation but continued as trustee.

For accreditation the American Bar Association required some day courses and at least 50 percent of the faculty teaching full time. Though Oregon's Supreme Court granted certification, the school's degrees lacked standing before the bar associations in other states. The idea of merger rose frequently as the trustees attempted to meet ABA requirements. Cramped quarters in the Giesy Building, the need to expand library holdings, and the pride of the hundreds of graduates who had passed the bar, practiced law, or served as Oregon judges further dictated action. The time was right, and in 1965 Northwestern College of Law, like Albany College, turned toward the southwest hills of Portland and a new beginning.

Two venerable institutions–Albany College and Northwestern College of Law–were nurtured by the communities which had given them life. Both had worked at molding character. Albany College had inculcated Christian values and offered work in the classics, music, arts, business, and science. Its students labored to develop strong bodies and informed minds. Its teachers exhorted them to be stewards of their talents, resources, and spiritual commitments. Northwestern College of Law, the state's first formal program of legal education, tapped the talent of members of the bar to teach new generations the intricacies of concise construction and argument. Students confirmed their skills in bar examinations, legal practice, and service in the courts. The melding of these institutions' histories suggested a common destiny and the prospect of distinction.

We are logically and ideally positioned
to develop the environmental curriculum and
programs relating to international business
transactions. It would help the Northwest get more
seriously involved in the Pacific Rim. That is
really the economic future of the Northwest.

DEAN STEPHEN KANTER
Northwestern School of Law, Lewis & Clark College
The Advocate, 1986

▲ Former Japanese Prime Minister Yasuhiro Nakasone visits with Stephen Kanter, dean and professor of law, and President Mooney in the faculty law library. The Northwestern School of Law has hosted numerous important visitors at various College functions— dedications, alumni day, and commencements. Speakers have included William O. Douglas, supreme court justice, 1970; Elliot Richardson, secretary of commerce, 1976; Griffin Bell, attorney general, 1978; and Anatoly Sobchak, mayor of Leningrad, 1990.

▲ Law enrollment began to reflect the changing demography of the 1980s, when enrollment of women students approached 40 percent of the entering class. Students concentrate on criminal law, taught by Professor Bill Williamson, below right. ▶ In 1967 the College purchased twenty acres near the junction of Terwilliger and Boones Ferry roads. In 1970 the law school moved from downtown Portland to its new permanent home. On a portion of the tract, the College developed Joe Huston Field, used for baseball, softball, and soccer.

◄ Dedicated in 1970, the Paul L. Boley Library houses Oregon's largest legal research collection. Other facilities opened that year included Gantenbein Student Lounge and the Chester E. McCarty Classroom Complex. Paul Thiry, Seattle architect, designed the initial buildings for the law campus. ▼ The terraced plaza of the law school campus, designed by Broome Oringdulph & O'Toole, is a hub of activity and is the site of a memorial sundial honoring former Oregon governor Tom McCall, champion of environmental issues.

FIR ACRES

To create a work of art challenges human ingenuity. Whether it be the nimble fingers of a Plains Indian woman fixing porcupine quill embroidery to a leather shirt, a Renaissance portrait painter bringing to life the humanity of his subject, or a Japanese gardener raking gravel into contemplative designs in a temple landscape—the human imagination draws on the creative impulse to produce something expressive and evocative. One great test is to merge functional design and decorative art. To marry function and decoration and to integrate all into nature is truly a rite of passage. A select few display the talent to craft a masterpiece.

In the mid-1920s, Herman Brookman, an architect-artist, crafted such a union when he imagined what might happen to a forested hillside near the Willamette River in the suburbs of Portland, Oregon. Brookman mirrored the enthusiasms of an interesting era in American architecture. Heavily influenced by historicism and committed to the ideals of the Arts and Crafts Movement, many artisans made a commitment to total design. In dreams and practice they sought to understand and work with the contours of the land and the colors bequeathed by nature. They designed for detail and demanded quality materials and craftsmanship. Their aims were harmony, beauty, and permanence. Brookman was of their fraternity.

In many ways, John Ruskin served as their mentor. In *The Seven Lamps of Architecture*, Ruskin celebrated the Gothic ideals and the mystery echoed in medieval European building. He also laid out a philosophy to nurture a new generation of designers. "Architecture," Ruskin wrote, "is the art which so disposes and adorns the edifices raised by man, for whatsoever uses, that the sight of them may contribute to his mental health, power, and pleasure." In the essay entitled "The Lamp of Memory," Ruskin asserted: "It is one of those moral duties . . . to build our dwellings with care, and patience, and fondness, and diligent competition, and with a view to their duration. . . ." Houses, concluded Ruskin, should "stand as long as human work at its strongest can be hoped to stand; recording to their children what they had been, and from what, if so it had been permitted, they had risen."

The achievement of these goals took time and money. Only the elite could afford such patronage. Herman Brookman catapulted himself into that world by sheer determination and talent. Born in 1891 in a Jewish neighborhood in Brooklyn, he grew up in a family with an ethic of striving. His immigrant parents saw America as a promised land where their children might grow without the atrocities of pogroms. New York nurtured the Brookmans, and Herman found a setting to grow as a designer. In 1906 he joined the architectural firm of Allbro and Lindeberg as an apprentice. Known for their work in designing country estates, the team drew heavily on Ruskin's ideals and the designs of Edwin Lutyens.

A British architect in his prime at the turn of the twentieth century, Lutyens gained considerable attention when in 1896 he designed a house at Munstead Wood near Godalming, England, for his cousin Gertrude Jekyll. In this project, Lutyens used stone, brick, weathered oak, and slate. He also worked closely with Jekyll, a woman whose skills in landscape design became legendary.

◄ *The Manor House, built for the Lloyd Frank family in 1925, is the campus centerpiece.* ▲ *The Fir Acres rose gardens drew wide acclaim.*

By 1900 Lutyens commanded a sizable following and obtained commissions to design romantic country houses. Lutyens prescribed dominant roofs, bold chimneys, variant fenestration, and an asymmetrical massing of forms. He drew inspiration from history but was not slavish in his use of design elements from the past.

The intellectual ties between the work of Lutyens and Jekyll and the work of Allbro and Lindeberg are clear. All drank from the same cup of inspiration, and it is likely that the American firm, either through visits or study of photographs and plans, grew by its awareness of the masterful designs for turn-of-the-century British estates. Herman Brookman flourished in this atmosphere and, in 1914, joined Harry Lindeberg in a new firm.

The Arts and Crafts Movement—driven by the philosophy, writing, and designs of William Morris—inspired not only architecture and landscape planning but also publishing, bookbinding, furniture design, pottery, and other decorative arts. In California the brothers Charles Sumner Greene and Henry Mather Greene jettisoned the eclecticism of the Queen Anne style of the 1890s to champion the shingled bungalow as a regional vernacular style wherein they executed total design: the building, furniture, light fixtures, and landscape. The celebration of hand craftsmanship in a machine age; bonding of metal, wood, and glass into harmonious designs; experimentation with glazed tiles; integrating works of art into structures; and transforming structures into works of art captured the interest of a generation of artisans and patrons.

Lloyd Frank, the heir to the mercantile fortune of his Jewish grandparents, worked in the early 1900s as the furniture buyer for Portland's Meier & Frank department store. A man of artistic temperament and acute sensitivity to quality, Frank took delight in the works of the Arts and Crafts period. So enamored was he with this artistry that he committed a substantial fortune to help realize a remarkable West Coast statement to that ideal—the creation and construction of the estate, Fir Acres, on Palatine Hill. Frank had the fortune and daring; Brookman, his chosen architect, had brought years of experience and imagination. Learning that Brookman might consider a West Coast commission, in 1923 Frank cabled him in Europe, where he was studying country estates and pursuing a lifelong interest in painting pastels. The offer was irresistible; within a few months Herman and Sophie Brookman moved to Portland. Brookman was ready to execute his masterpiece and Frank was prepared to pay whatever it cost.

The names Meier and Frank confirmed what hard work and opportunity might accomplish on the Oregon frontier. In 1855 Aaron Meier emigrated from Germany to join his brothers in their general merchandise store during the gold rush in Downieville, California. Sensing the potential for returns on labor, Meier set out as an itinerant peddler into the mines of the upper Klamath country and the Rogue River Valley, selling needles, thread, buttons, and whatever he could carry in his pack. In 1857 Meier opened a small dry goods store in Portland, then a community of about thirteen hundred residents. Meier's choice of location proved wise, for though he faced stiff competition, Portland rapidly emerged as a regional crossroads city. It drew the agricultural products of the Willamette Valley, the shipping of the world, and—after 1862—a steady flow of bullion from the mines of the Boise Basin, Orofino and Florence, John Day country, and elsewhere in the interior.

Meier returned to Germany in 1863, married Jeanette Hirsch, and—armed with $14,000, his share in his family estate—returned to

▲ From 1942 to 1952, the Gatehouse served as the residence for Morgan and Ruth Odell, and subsequently was used as a men's dormitory and various administrative offices. ▶ The tapestry and sideboard are original pieces from the Frank family given to the College by Edna Frank Holmes during her long tenure as a trustee.

We did not have any idea what
we wanted to build,
but we wanted something appropriate
for the property.

EDNA FRANK HOLMES
interview with Bruce Abbott, 1973

The plan comes first, offering comfort, convenience, pleasure; then the relations of the natural surroundings of site or garden. From this foundation, the style and external detail of the finished structure should rise as a monument to the beauty of architectural expression.

HERMAN BROOKMAN
Fir Acres architect, 1924

Portland to resume his business at 136 Front Street. The Meiers did not prosper immediately. They literally had to begin their business anew and endured periods of adversity and nightmares about securing credit. They persevered and slowly expanded. In 1870 Aaron Meier invited Emil Frank of San Francisco to join him as a clerk. Frank became a partner in 1873 and brought his brother, Sigmund, to the store in Portland. The younger Frank, a musician born in Germany, taught violin and piano in New York to pay for his travel to the West Coast. In 1885 Sigmund Frank married Fannie Meier, eldest daughter of Aaron and Jeanette Meier, and, in 1887, replaced his brother as the principal partner in the family store.

Aaron Meier died in 1889. His business skills had laid the foundation for a family dynasty; his widow, Jeanette, ruled it with love and determination for the next thirty-six years. Sigmund Frank served as chief executive until his death in 1910; however, his mother-in-law went to the store every day and exercised unerring control of its affairs until her death in 1925. Then, by the terms of her will, she sought through her "earnest wish and prayer" that her heirs would carry on "the great enterprise initiated by my husband."

Eventually Meier & Frank became the region's largest department store. In 1898 the family erected a new building with two elevators on Fifth Avenue between Alder and Morrison. In 1909 they added a ten-story annex to cope with expanding business. In 1914 they razed the first wing to build a sixteen-story structure which catapulted Meier & Frank to the fourth-largest department store in the United States. Lloyd Frank, eldest son of Sigmund and Fannie (Meier) Frank, managed the furniture department and served as treasurer. Aaron Frank, his brother, handled day-to-day business affairs. Abraham Meier, their uncle, served from 1910 to 1930 as titular president and "greeter" of the public. Julius Meier, another uncle, worked as general manager until 1930 when he became governor of Oregon.

Family and fortune encircled the heirs of the Meier & Frank venture, yet all did not march to the same cadence nor achieve the harmony Jeanette Meier earnestly insisted upon in her last instructions to her children and grandchildren. In 1915 Lloyd met and, after a whirlwind courtship of three months, married Edna Levy of San Francisco. The daughter of a successful wholesale jeweler and educated at Miss Murrison's School, Edna moved to Portland to join her husband's family in celebrating the opening of their new store in the heart of the city's burgeoning commercial district. "Ye gads, a one-track town," was Edna's first reaction, but she learned to like Portland and discovered its amenities.

The Franks had three children: Fred, born in 1916; Dorothy, born in 1918; and Margery, born in 1923. By 1920 Lloyd and Edna Frank had decided to find a country location for a family home. She preferred a waterfront site, but, when Lloyd took her out Taylor's Ferry Road to a tract of sixty-three acres on a hillside facing toward Mount Hood, she felt they need look no farther. That he had already purchased this portion of the William Torrance donation land claim closed the matter anyway. Logged in the nineteenth century, the acreage had reforested in Douglas fir interspersed with groves of maple and alder. A spring, bubbling to the surface not far from the crest of the ridge, gave the assurance of a steady water supply even though the property lay beyond the city's lines.

The stage was set: a young couple of ample means with a growing family wanted to build a country residence. A New York architect with nearly two decades of experience in designing quality homes awaited a patron to fund his imagination. Thus fortune turned

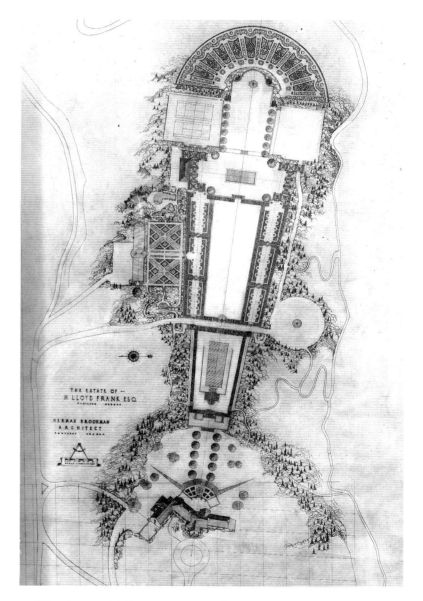

◄ The forested hills of southwest Portland embrace the 130 acres of Lewis & Clark College. Although nearly seven decades have passed, Herman Brookman's imprint for the Fir Acres landscape remains largely intact. ▲ Herman Brookman's site plan for Fir Acres in 1924 complemented the natural setting of the property, with five terraces for formal grounds and unique water features.

toward friendship when, in 1923, Oscar Bach of New York, a skilled artist in metalwork and acquaintance of Frank, recommended Herman Brookman. The timing was right; Brookman agreed to Frank's offer. The Franks gave him virtually free hand to do what he wanted. "We did not have any idea what we wanted to build," recalled Edna, "but we wanted something appropriate for the property." Brookman understood. Before he was finished in 1926 his patrons had expended $1,300,000 on Fir Acres.

Herman Brookman began with a survey to orient Fir Acres on an east-west axis focused upon Mount Hood on the distant horizon. Crews felled trees, blasted stumps, and commenced wresting roots from the spongy soil to open the vista. Ultimately the designs required more than one hundred sheets, each meticulously drawn to prescribe dimensions, materials, and decorative detail. Brookman operated with a simple philosophy: "The plan comes first, offering comfort, convenience, pleasure; then the relations of the natural surroundings of site or garden. From this foundation, the style and external detail of the finished structure should rise as a monument to the beauty of architectural expression."

The Fir Acres estate included a complex of buildings and landscape design. On the western margin of the property, Brookman envisioned a gatehouse in the English cottage style. This romantic stone building with a slate roof suggested the presence of something grand but not quite revealed. The residence, barely visible through the stone buttresses at the estate entry, stood on the brow of the ridge in a clearing of selectively thinned Douglas fir and maple.

Brookman designed a rambling, asymmetrical building of two and a half stories plus a half basement. From the foundation upward the architect designed for permanence. The crews of McHolland Builders laid a dozen inches of crushed gravel, poured a four-inch concrete slab, and then placed another inch of concrete. On this foundation rose three rectangular units, irregularly placed, but with a central section mounting through the firs with a dramatic, steeply-pitched roof. To foster a sense of belonging and age, Brookman prescribed offsetting the timbers in the attic to craft undulations in the roof as if settling and passage of time had shaped the feature. To accentuate height and draw the eye upward, he ordered that the Pennsylvania slates change from large to small as they ascended the framing. To fix all permanently, he insisted on copper wires to hold the heavy slates to the supporting timbers.

Unusual in the Pacific Northwest where wood frame construction dominated domestic architecture, Brookman decided to build with brick. The choice of this material, use of ornamental lintels of hand-carved oak, and design of windows with leaded glass, colored panes, and intricate metal grills bonded the building to the country houses of such masters as Edwin Lutyens in Great Britain. Brookman was determined to produce precisely the right effect. To achieve it he made repeated trips to the clay pits and kilns at the Willamina Brickworks in Yamhill County where he watched the firings and personally selected pallets of brick for shipment to Portland.

Then, during on-site supervision, he instructed masons on color selection and laying of bricks to obtain the patterns and textures in the Arts and Crafts tradition. Brookman had the men lay clinkers, turn bricks on edge, create herringbone designs, form headers of dark bricks, set others to project on the building's towers, and craft light lattice designs on the walls of the gables. He used rough-dressed stone for three squared buttresses on the west elevation and decorative work around the children's entrance to the left of the main entry. Handcrafted lead gutters with four-inch downspouts extended along the eaves to handle the Oregon rains which annually drenched the property.

Those who passed the gatehouse and proceeded toward the residence's main entry encountered a deeply recessed vestibule surmounted by an oak lintel carved with entwined mythological beasts, a wrought-iron balcony, and a handcrafted, hanging metal light fixture. To the right, in a niche surrounded by carved oak, reposed "Blue Belle," an Art Deco statue. Beside the massive entry door was the Mezuzah containing the Hebrew words of the "Great Commandment" from Deuteronomy:

> *Hear, O Israel: The Lord our God is one Lord: And thou shalt love the Lord thy God with all thine heart, and with all thy soul, and with all thy might.*
> *And these words, which I command thee this day, shall be in thine heart:*
> *And thou shalt teach them diligently unto thy children, and shalt talk of them when thou sittest in thine house, and when thou walkest by the way, and when thou liest down, and when thou risest up.*
> *And thou shalt bind them for a sign upon thine hand, and they shall be as frontlets between thine eyes.*

On the east elevation facing the Cascade Range, Brookman planned a generous flagstone terrace for which he designed teak garden benches and created round wooden tubs with metal bands for plantings. On the building exterior he placed a menagerie of animals: a pair of imperial eagles, two cross-eyed owls, a stunning metal water buffalo's head beneath a projecting oriel window, and stone Cambodian Fu dogs which he and Lloyd Frank found on a trip to San Francisco. Beyond these sculptural pieces, Oscar Bach worked animals and flowers into the metal tracery of window screens for the first floor, while Roi Morin executed a number of carvings in the massive seasoned-oak lintels.

Brookman celebrated craftsman ideals with greater intensity in the principal rooms on the first floor of the residence. Oak paneling and carvings of ivy, flowers, human portrait cameos, gargoyle-like visages, and fans of peacock feathers in the top sections of bookcases in the pine-paneled library provided a dark, almost somber statement in fine-grained wood. Mythological sea creatures, cast in the plaster ceiling of the two-story stair hall where a circular staircase floated against a massive wall of mullioned windows, provided a lighter atmosphere. Brookman also prescribed custom screens for the seven fireplaces; laid out patterning for cork flooring at the children's entry; and designed alternating wide and narrow, pegged hardwood flooring for major rooms. The rambling house of more than thirty rooms included a sunken living room, dining room, octagonal breakfast room, reception hall, library, children's playroom, master suite with adjacent sitting room, a dozen other bedrooms, several bathrooms, servants' quarters, garage bays, and basement rooms for wine storage, laundry, ironing, and a steam boiler for heating the building. Hidden behind handsome oak doors, a three-story elevator rose from the basement to the servants' quarters beneath the attic.

Except for Henry Pittock's mansion in the West Hills, a structure erected in 1906, Portland had no other home so grand. From the months of its construction in 1924-25, the residence looked like it belonged. The exterior walls of buff bricks, gray-stained oak lintels, and rugged roof slates settled in comfortably to the foggy mornings,

*After all, it's my house and he's building it
for me. I can't criticize Brookman
for building it as well as he knows how.*

LLOYD FRANK
speaking of Herman Brookman, 1924

▲ In July 1925, workmen completed construction of the Frank family's home. Their heaviest labor involved placing 180 tons of roof slates which had been shipped in six boxcars from Pennsylvania.

▲ Lush plantings soften the cobblestones at the entrance of the
Fir Acres estate service buildings, circa 1930. The water fountain
made a unique focal point. ▶ Originally four in number, the three
remaining sculpted dolphins grace the walkway near BoDine Hall.

misty rainy seasons, and stands of majestic firs on the ridge above the Willamette River.

To the eastern vista, totally hidden from the distant Palatine Hill Road, Brookman laid out one of the grandest formal landscapes in Oregon. Rivaled only by the botanical gardens on the coastal estate of Louis J. Simpson on the cliffs south of Coos Bay, the grounds consisted of a series of terraces dropping gracefully down the hill with a rigid geometrical axis aligning house, pools, lawns, gazebos, flagpole, and rose beds with Mount Hood. The effect was stunning, for Brookman left a fringe of conifers and planted Norway spruce to soften the bounds of the terraces, designed rough-dressed stone walls, and laid out a series of water features. Water drawn from the springhouse to an underground reservoir flowed from a fountain and cascaded down a stepped waterfall into a large reflecting pool. More water flowed from the Gorgon fountain into a small fish pond, and at yet another terrace a large swimming pool surrounded by imported white sand lay between matching massive grape arbors. To the north stood the bath house; to the south was the barbecue area. Beneath the lowest terrace lay rose beds, holding, by the late 1920s, several thousand bushes. The rose gardens at Fir Acres exceeded the famed plantings in Portland's Washington Park.

Brookman designed a system of meandering roadways of Belgian cobblestones. Construction at Fir Acres coincided with the removal of several blocks of cobblestones between First and Third avenues on the Portland waterfront. Truckloads of the stones moved out Corbett, Virginia, and Taylor's Ferry roads to the estate on Palatine Hill. Brookman further prescribed extensive plantings of foxglove backed by dense thickets of rhododendrons to fill in between the margins of the roadways and the nearby forest.

The grounds included a pair of tennis courts of short-clipped grass north of the gardens, a bowling green on the fourth terrace—where no one ever bowled—a whimsical rock garden, and a glass-domed conservatory for tropical plants. That building gained Oscar Bach's signature piece for the estate, the handsome wrought-iron monkey door singled out for its "gentle savagery" by *Country Life* in 1932 in an essay on the "Glorious Gardens on the Estate of Lloyd Frank, Esq." Nearby ran bed upon bed of cutting gardens providing a succession of narcissus, daffodils, tulips, and annuals.

Brookman also designed service buildings, a three-sided complex with bays for tractors, extra automobiles, farm equipment, refrigeration rooms for holding cut flowers, and upstairs quarters for workers on the grounds. He designed the clock tower which surmounted the central two-story unit of this complex and prescribed an elegant dovecote with a massive weathervane atop the gardeners' workroom. The south unit of the complex was a hulking greenhouse with a glass roof. Two other greenhouses, a bit smaller, stood beside it. This complex faced west into a central courtyard beyond which Brookman placed a small fountain with four spouting dolphins.

Brookman "was more than an architect," said his son. "He was a very artistic person who would not tolerate shoddiness in others. He was hard on those who worked for him but could be kind as well." At Fir Acres he had key associates. Roi Morin, who carved some of the notable wood sculptural pieces in the residence, served as principal assistant and draftsman. Oscar Bach executed a number of commissions for metalwork including the oriel window above the eastern terrace, the monkey door in the conservatory, and the balcony over the main entrance. Fred Baker, a craftsman in electrical fixtures, designed and constructed special lamps in the gardens and interior and exterior lights for the buildings. Through these kindred spirits

and in his daily monitoring of construction, "Brooky," as the Franks fondly began calling him, achieved the ideals of the Arts and Crafts Movement. As Ruskin had suggested, a house should "stand as long as human work at its strongest can be hoped to stand." In that Brookman met every test.

Life at Fir Acres proved more fragile, though for a time all was well. Thirty-four servants cared for the five members of the Frank family and the sprawling estate. The staff included an upstairs maid, downstairs maid, cook, cook's helper, butler, chauffeur and two laundresses who coped with the washing for all who resided on the property. The head gardener, formerly of Kew Gardens in London, lived with his family in the gatehouse, while others on staff occupied the top floor of the main residence or apartments in the service buildings adjacent to the greenhouses. Smith, the head gardener, proved highly temperamental. "He wouldn't let me pick flowers," recalled Edna Frank Holmes in later years. "He'd come up in the morning and say, 'What flowers would you like, madam?'"

Even if the gardener did not want to permit the mistress of the estate to pick her own flowers, he labored diligently to turn the gardens, her special delight at Fir Acres, into a West Coast showplace. Within a year or two of moving to Fir Acres, the Franks hosted national meetings of the American Garden Club and the American Medical Association. The roses won medals, trophies and rave reviews. And, in time, the Franks hosted a series of charity events for the Boy Scouts, Girl Scouts, United Good Neighbors, and others. Opening the grounds had its costs, for gawkers tried to peer into the house. The staff maintained privacy by draping the living room windows with sheets during public events.

Edna Frank's interest in music led to a series of cultural events at Fir Acres. The Portland Junior Symphony played on the terrace, as guests sat on the lawn facing the residence. The London String Quartet also performed at the estate. And her friend, virtuoso pianist Arthur Rubinstein, later recounted in his autobiography his misadventure during a journey to Fir Acres. Rubinstein, ever the romeo, leaned over to steal a kiss from the "beautiful Edna" who was driving one of the family's Oldsmobiles. "She let go of the wheel and closed her eyes," recalled Rubinstein, "and the car with us inside, fell on its side into the thick snow. We climbed out rather painfully and the new situation looked rather grim. 'What shall we do?' I asked nervously, thinking of my train and her husband. She answered, 'You must run down and ask for help. There is a garage at the bottom of the road.'" After hiking through the snow, Rubinstein eventually found assistance. "It took us a dreadful three hours to get safely back to town. Fortunately we returned before alarming the husband and missing my train," he noted. Even when she was past ninety, Edna delighted in telling of this incident, as did *Time* magazine, which featured it as a sidebar in its 1980 review of Rubinstein's *My Many Years*.

Fred, Dorothy, and Margery Frank had special adventures. Just inside the children's entrance their parents installed a soda fountain. The nearby pantry yielded a steady supply of ice cream and made their back corner of the house a haunt for friends. They slid down the narrow banister in the front stair hallway, hid treasures in the secret drawer in the twelfth step, rode astride a stuffed horse (of real horsehair) on wheels, explored the woods, and watched the garden crews laboring with the work horses. In the evenings they gathered in the living room to load rolls into the baby grand player piano or

stroke the electrical Thuraman, an instrument with an exposed wire which produced strange tones especially appealing to children.

The Franks also hosted a number of parties. In the summer of 1932 the Portland Junior Symphony held a fund-raiser at Fir Acres. The staff laid a wooden dance floor in the large cobblestone circle adjacent to the gardens and ringed it with booths serving food or offering games of chance. Friends and patrons gathered for two days and listened to evening concerts by the sixty-member orchestra. For a number of years the Franks held a private New Year's Eve party with Rabbi Henry Berkowitz dressed as Father Time and Lloyd Frank outfitted as Baby New Year. "Then at midnight," recalled Edna, "we'd all go down to the flagpole in the garden and salute the flag. We did some crazy things back then."

In spite of family, wealth, and position, however, Lloyd Frank grew dissatisfied. Gradually two groups of friends appeared at Fir Acres: those associated with Edna's cultural and gardening interests or the children, and his friends, who often gathered around the pool. After a while Edna ordered a brass telescope from the store and used it to look down toward the pool to assess whether the visitors were "his friends" or "my friends." "If I liked them, I'd go down," she said; "if I didn't, I'd stay home."

The Franks separated, then divorced. Lloyd left Portland, twice remarried, and died in 1959. Left with three children on the palatial estate in the midst of the Great Depression, Edna had to decide what to do. One thing was certain—she could not maintain a household which included thirty-four servants. To provide for her and the children the family eventually settled on trusts with control vested in the hands of Aaron Frank, Lloyd's brother and emerging major figure in the 1930s in the Meier & Frank store.

Edna, Fred, Dorothy, and Margery Frank left Fir Acres in 1935 for a home near Washington Park in the southwest hills of Portland. "I would have loved to stay," said Edna, "but by that time I was in love again—so who cares about a house." She married W. H. "Ted" Holmes and lived for a number of years in a country house by the Willamette River in Wilsonville. Fred Frank died in a plane crash in 1942, while training pilots near La Grande, Oregon. Dorothy Frank graduated from Mills College and married Lester Sherman. Margery Frank married Capt. Lewis Russell and later married John Crist, a retired sociology professor from Lewis & Clark College.

Herman Brookman remained in Oregon for nearly forty years. In 1927 he played a central role in designing Temple Beth Israel, a masterpiece which drew upon Byzantine themes. The structure housed a cavernous one thousand-seat auditorium, surmounted by a double dome with walls lit by luminescent bays of windows. In spite of the economic difficulties of the 1930s, Brookman found steady work as an architect specializing in residential design. Never again, however, did he secure a commission like that which came with Lloyd Frank's cable inviting him to work in Portland. Brookman died in California in 1973.

Edna Holmes returned many times to Fir Acres. In 1945 she became a trustee of Lewis & Clark College and served for more than three decades. She then continued as an active life trustee. The College named the Edna Holmes Terrace on the east side of the mansion in her honor, for there she had taken special pleasure in sunny days and in hosting memorable musical programs. Alert and fit until her ninety-fifth year, Edna Holmes was a beloved mother, grandmother, and great grandmother—and to a college, an enduring friend in its new history on Palatine Hill. Edna Holmes died on June 17, 1990.

▲ By the summer of 1926, the work crews had transformed the forest into a grand formal landscape. Extensive plantings of ornamental shrubs and rosebushes defined the perimeter of the grounds. The Gatehouse originally served as the home of the estate gardener. Edna Frank with her children, Dorothy and Fred. Her third child, Margery, was born subsequent to the photograph.

This is the place of pure invention . . .

PROFESSOR VERN RUTSALA
"The World," *The New Life*, 1978

Lewis & Clark College

▲ "We used a band of sheep in lieu of lawn mowers. Seven sheep were obtained and placed at first in the tennis courts. The original clay courts had grown over with grass and weeds, and it did not take the hungry band long to clear it off. Then with the portable fencing we moved them into successive small areas . . . till we finally got them up on the lawns around the mansion house." – Professor Benjamin A. Thaxter, about the College's early years at the estate.
▶ The Lion's Head is one of the water features in the landscape.

◄ Jonathon Horn, '79, and Reed Elwyn, '79, wrote a nomination to list parts of the College on the National Register of Historic Places. In 1980, a federal grant facilitated restoration of the grape arbors.

▼ In 1942, Professor Benjamin Thaxter wrote of nature's efforts to reclaim the estate: "Wild mallards and watersnakes had taken over the reflecting pool and the swimming pool. Raccoons made their homes in the forested ravines. Skunks . . . visited the garbage cans nightly. Gophers, white-footed mice, moles, and shrews were abundant. The little Oregon weasel was sometimes seen and foxes and deer occasionally visited the tract. . . . Bird life was abundant."

I thought:
O God, the Church must have this!
It can be a citadel
of light and learning,
of faith and knowledge
for young people
and the world they can serve.

PRESIDENT MORGAN ODELL
reflecting in 1978 on his first visit
to Fir Acres estate in 1941

◄ In the early years at Fir Acres estate, more than thirty servants cared for the five members of the Frank family, and the Manor House and grounds were a focal point of Portland social life. ▲ The hanging lamp on the Gatehouse wall is one of many handcrafted by Frederick Baker, an electrical contractor and friend of Lloyd Frank.

He was more than an architect.
He was a very artistic person who
would not tolerate shoddiness in others.
He was hard on those who worked for him
but could be kind as well.

BERNARD BROOKMAN
regarding his father, Herman Brookman
Quoted by Paul Pintarich in *Oregonian*, 1974

▲ In the 1920s, Oscar Bach handcrafted several metal traceries for window screens on the first floor of the Manor. An ornamental heron adorns a door window at the main entrance. ▶ In 1991, the College refurbished Armstrong Lounge, the Manor's living room. The event honored the retirement of Edith Smith, a member of the faculty and staff from 1947-90, and reaffirmed the College's appreciation of the Armstrong family's generosity. The lounge was dedicated in 1948 to honor Mr. and Mrs. Thomas J. Armstrong, whose bequest assisted in Albany College's move to Fir Acres.

My people, now it is time
for us all to shake hands with the rain.
It's a neighbor, lives here all winter.

PROFESSOR WILLIAM E. STAFFORD
"Wovoka's Witness," *Stories That Could Be True,* 1977

◄ Generations of Lewis & Clark students have found the gazebos and grounds of the estate a quiet respite for reflection, interaction, and the building of memories. The reflecting pond in the foreground has served as a kangaroo court dunk tank in freshman hazings, a volleyball court, a skating pond during winter months, and as a cooling conduit for campus air conditioning systems.
▲ The lower campus awakens on a foggy November morning.

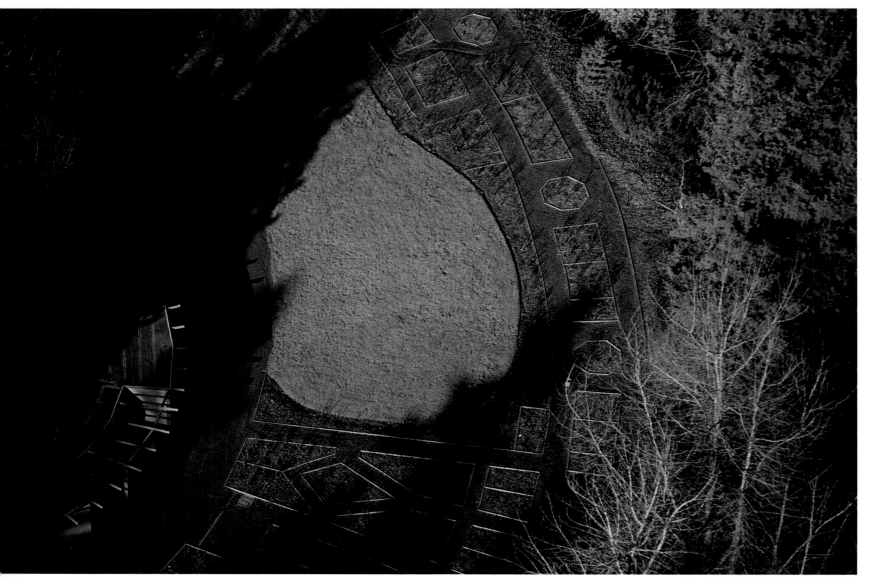

▲ In the 1940s, the Lewis & Clark College Rose Garden Club restored the original rose plantings as a memorial to students and faculty serving in World War II. Trustee Victor Creed, named life curator, inspired and coordinated volunteer efforts. ▶ Since 1942, Albany Quadrangle has served as a chapel, library, classrooms, and departmental offices. Original apple trees from the estate provide color and occasional sustenance for Summer School students.

As if unsure of its date,
the day begins slowly.

PROFESSOR VERN RUTSALA
"Today is Monday," *The Window*, 1964

COLLEGE ON PALATINE HILL

The near-death struggles of Albany College tried the souls of the faculty, trustees, alumni, and supporters. "To my very friends I am a spectacle of pity," said Prometheus, and such seemed the school's condition. Debt, declining enrollment, revocation of accreditation, the foundation of the Women's Building—nine years in the ground without a structure above—these were results of the 1930s. Yet "blind hope" glimmered: classes in Portland might save the College. Hope and hard work were part of the story. Faith, friendship, and leadership proved critical ingredients. In the 1940s the College found them, and, in time, it found a new destiny in Portland.

"We shall be as a city on a hill and all the eyes of the world shall be upon us," preached John Winthrop as his band of Pilgrim followers set foot in 1630 on the shores of Massachusetts Bay. That imagery inspired College leaders for years. Rev. Edward Geary, one of the founders, observed in 1867 that the Albany Collegiate Institute was to become "a beacon of light to the whole Northwest." In 1952 College president Morgan Odell opened the academic year with the text "a city set on a hill cannot be hid." Faith in what the College might become and vision that the labor was worth the investment inspired the community to transform a dream into reality.

By 1938 the changed circumstances were evident. Only six of thirty-six trustees resided in Albany. The Portland program, which first operated in the Allen Building at Southeast Twelfth and Salmon, moved into new quarters, the former Temple Beth Israel School. Merchant Aaron Frank had called to the trustees' attention this available, unoccupied, two-story brick building designed by Herman Brookman. The location was excellent. A few blocks west were the Portland Art Museum and the Multnomah County Library. The College leased Turnverein Hall for its gymnasium and the basement of the nearby Nazarene Church for a library.

As enrollment grew, the College expanded the curriculum in Portland from two years to four. In 1938 four critical needs faced the institution: a visionary president, accreditation, financial stability, and a new campus. In the interim, Clarence Greene, president in the 1920s, returned to the College, and in 1939, Benjamin Thaxter, a Yale graduate, was named dean. These men and others from the Albany campus provided four years of critical service to help meet these challenges.

As the Great Depression robbed the College of its lifeblood in the 1930s, American involvement in World War II in 1941 also threatened. As war efforts drew away male students, the College presented thirty-one graduates—the largest number in its history—and seized its opportunity. In contract with the Civil Aeronautics Administration, the mathematics department initiated courses in navigation and meteorology in the Civilian Pilot Training Program. Miss Bessie Holladay's School of Flying taught flight instruction. With Pearl Harbor, the College moved the CPTP to Ontario, Oregon. Wartime also permitted the trustees to rent the Monteith Campus to the U.S. Army and the National Youth Administration. In the months of transition from peace to war, the Board of Trustees adopted a policy on "Academic Tenure for the Albany College Faculty." The transition was under way and, in spite of world events, the school found the means to keep going.

◄ *The New Office Building was erected in 1963.* ▲ *The owl is presented in the Aubrey R. Watzek awards to leaders for service in the community.*

*There is already too much
black and white thinking —
theory/practice, feeling/thought,
new/conventional. We should aim for an
awareness of relations, contexts, processes.*

PROFESSOR JOHN BROWN
Dean of Faculty
Journal of Lewis & Clark, 1975

▲ In 1979 the Olin Foundation gave $4 million to construct the Olin
Physics and Chemistry Laboratory Building and purchase furnish-
ings and equipment. An additional $5 hundred thousand was raised
to complete the project. The facility includes an observatory with
Newtonian-style telescope, a seismograph, fifteen laboratories,
a machine shop, two lecture-demonstration amphitheaters, and
equipment for muon research, calorimetry, cryogenics, radioactive
monitoring, biochemistry, and spectroscopy. The stainless steel
double helix sculpture was crafted by Obie Simonis, visiting artist.

The search for a campus led Presbyterian leaders, trustees, and College officials to examine several possibilities. In 1940 the board launched a fund campaign to purchase twenty acres on Mount Tabor in Portland. Although the board obtained an option on the land, it raised only two-thirds of the necessary $32,500 before dropping the effort. Some argued for another site—the Lloyd Frank estate, Fir Acres. More than three times the size of the Mount Tabor property, Fir Acres possessed buildings, tennis courts, and a swimming pool, plus room for expansion. The College's $20,000, however, seemed so insignificant against the Frank family's investment of $1,300,000 during the 1920s that nothing came of the interest—at first.

In finding a new president the College had more ready success. Morgan Odell was known to West Coast Presbyterians as a popular professor at Occidental College in Los Angeles. He had graduated from that college in 1917, served in World War I, labored as minister of Christian education for the First Methodist Church in Pasadena, and in 1931 received his doctorate at the University of Chicago. Odell possessed a strong personality, an enormous capacity for work, and an uncanny ability to persuade others to make dreams happen. In November 1941 Odell came to Portland to interview for the post of president and to meet Aaron Frank to discuss the prospects of securing Fir Acres for a new campus.

Frank's awareness of Albany College's situation had deepened since the lease of the Temple Beth Israel School. In 1940 trustees Herbert Templeton and C. W. Platt had talked with Frank about giving to the fund drive for the Mount Tabor property. Frank turned them down but indicated he might assist if they sought a campus on the west side of the Willamette River. He thus gave the subtle signal that as trustee of his brother Lloyd's assets, including Fir Acres, he might entertain an offer for the property. As the board focused on Odell as its presidential candidate, Harry Bruck, chairman, and C. W. Platt, secretary, again visited Aaron Frank and stated that the College had a strong interest in Fir Acres but could pay only $50,000. Frank said he would accept that sum, provided the board found the right president. The meeting between Frank and Odell in November 1941 proved pivotal. "He is your man. Don't let him get away from us. We need him in Portland," Frank told the trustees.

The events of November and December 1941 were a turning point in the institution's history. The trustees succeeded in finding a highly motivated educator to consider assuming the day-to-day administration of an unaccredited college operating in rented buildings and burdened with debt. The meeting of Morgan Odell with Aaron Frank and the evident support of trustees Templeton and Platt raised the tantalizing possibility of obtaining the new campus. Even the plunge of the United States into the war on December 7 did not stay the course. Three days later the trustees offered Odell the presidency. A calculated risk-taker, he accepted.

Odell laid out conditions for coming to Portland. The trustees and presbytery must meet $7,500 in unpaid faculty salaries, provide for a 38 percent increase in salaries for the coming school year, and purchase Fir Acres. They accepted and hired Odell under a one-year contract with the prospect of renewed employment. They announced his appointment, the pending purchase of Fir Acres, the opportunity of friends to visit the estate, and a crash fund-raising campaign to purchase the campus and pay the salaries.

The Albany College Women's League agreed to forgive $8,000 in notes held against debt on the Monteith Campus and turned over all their assets—$4,000 in cash and $2,000 in college bonds—to the project. With two days to go, the trustees had $33,000 in cash, but

even when Frank cut the price to $46,000, they were short of what they needed. Odell and trustee Lorne Miller then called on E. B. McNaughton of the First National Bank, presented their case, and borrowed $13,000 for ninety days. On June 30, with anticipation and optimism, the trustees closed the purchase.

Aaron Frank's willingness to work with the trustees and Odell proved crucial. A Jewish merchant, over a period of four years, had gently helped move a troubled Presbyterian college toward a new beginning. The news reverberated throughout Oregon. Keepers of the faith—the small student body, College staff, alumni, Oregon Presbyterians, and friends—saw their hope sustained.

The summer of 1942 proved remarkable. College staff explored the mansion, discussed uses and modifications for estate buildings, and examined the grounds. During the seven years Fir Acres had languished as an unsold property, ivy had escaped planting beds to wrap around shrubs, trees, and lamp posts. Shrubbery nearly enveloped the gazebos, concealed the great stone walls, and served as home to wild animals. Plantings around the residence had grown to conceal its exterior features, while the healthy deodar cedars started to block the once-panoramic vista of Mount Hood and the Cascade Range. The staff and students, including two of Odell's pupils from Occidental, spent eight hectic weeks transforming the wild landscape and structures into usable facilities for the opening of fall term.

Dean Benjamin Thaxter and Lucius McAfee worked with the students to convert the service building's north wing—once used for automobile repair—into a new chapel. Volunteers cleaned the reflecting and swimming pools. Crews sawed boards and built shelving for the Wallace Howe Lee Library, named in honor of a beloved Albany College president, professor, and generous donor of books. Others set up tables in the dining room on the main floor of the house which was to become the new College commons.

A sense of pioneering gripped those shaping the new campus on Palatine Hill Road. In 1940 President Greene had referred to "Lewis & Clark College" as a possible name for a transformed institution. In 1942, to herald the opening of the new campus, the trustees adopted the name, Lewis & Clark College. "The sterling character of these men and their valuable services to the country in appraising the resources of the region," noted the resolution, "and their blazing a trail for the thousands of sturdy pioneers to follow, would be certain to provide inspiration to our college." While their understanding of the route taken by Lewis and Clark was mistaken in connecting it with the subsequent Oregon Trail, the trustees grasped the symbolic importance of the new name.

Meriwether Lewis and William Clark breathed the spirit of the Enlightenment in the vast American West. With courage, they undertook Jefferson's assignment to explore, map, describe, and collect examples of the region's resources. From Indian word lists and basketry to collections of flora and fauna, they carried out their labors. They took temperatures of hot springs, determined longitude and latitude of landmarks, observed the weather, and succeeded in leading their crew—including Sacajawea and her infant son—to the Pacific. In a very real sense commitments of the College mirrored the explorers' breadth of assignment and work.

Above all, there was the matter of character. The quality of both men as leaders and human beings resounded through their diaries and field notes. For example, on August 18, 1805, when nearing the crest of the Rockies on the westward journey, Meriwether Lewis reflected on his birthday and the meaning of life:

Wisdom is having things right in your life
and knowing why.
If you do not have things right in your life,
you will be overwhelmed:
you may be heroic,
but you will not be wise.

PROFESSOR WILLIAM E. STAFFORD
"The Little Ways That Encourage Good Fortune"
Stories That Could Be True, 1977

◄ Carved in cedar by Lelooska and cast in concrete, this sculpture is one of four on the bridge leading into Agnes Flanagan Chapel. It depicts the winged eagle, representing the evangelist John, who stressed the oneness of Christ with God. The eagle holds the sun, protecting it as it lights the world. Other sculptures include the winged man, denoting Matthew; the winged lion, symbolizing Mark; and the winged ox, representing Luke. ▲ Named in honor of Aubrey R. Watzek, the library designed by Paul Thiry draws on Northwest Indian plank houses to define its series of pavilions.

Music fills the air whether it be from
a combo . . . piano or records,
Converse or dance,
It's all fun in the shack.

Voyageur, 1954

▲ The Snack Shack was the hub of student activities until 1958, when Templeton College Center was built. The building was later used as the library annex and lecture hall before demolition in 1980.

This day I completed my thirty-first year, and conceived that I had in all human probability now existed about half the period which I am to remain in this Sublunary world. I reflected that I had as yet done but little, very little indeed, to further the happiness of the human race or to advance the information of the succeeding generation. I viewed with regret the many hours I have spent in indolence, and now soarly feel the want of that information which those hours would have given me had they been judiciously expended, but since they are past and cannot be recalled, I dash from me the gloomy thought, and resolved in future, to redouble my exertions and at least indeavour to promote those two primary objects of human existence, by giving them the aid of that portion of talents which nature and fortune have bestoed on me; or in future, to live for mankind, as I have heretofore lived for myself.

Lewis & Clark College opened in September 1942, its student body depleted by the war but determined to proceed. The Frank residence became the Women's Building, named for the Women's League, who had helped secure the property. The structure housed two classrooms, dining commons and social rooms, the dean of women, and a women's dormitory for thirty residents. The service buildings became the Albany Quadrangle. It housed the Copeland Memorial Chapel, library, chemistry and physics laboratories, six classrooms, and two faculty apartments. Crews transformed the conservatory into the biology department with classrooms, lab, and greenhouse on the upper story and a dormitory for fifteen men on the first floor. The Odells moved into the gatehouse. Students planted victory gardens and produced everything from vegetables to rhubarb for the campus. "At last our dream has come true!" proclaimed the *Lewis and Clark College Bulletin* in October.

Operating on a semester system with 124 credit hours required for graduation, the College offered courses in nineteen departments distributed through four divisions: Humanities, Natural Sciences and Mathematics, Social Sciences, and Education. Courses offered included a dozen majors—from Art or History and Government to Music, Physics, Mathematics, and Physical Education for Men. The *Oregonian* gave coverage to Portland's "Cinderella College" and *Time* magazine called Lewis & Clark a "Courageous College."

The imprint of Odell's presidency surfaced on the first day of classes. Determined to gain accreditation as quickly as possible, Odell had recruited several new faculty members, including A. A. Groening, professor of physics and mathematics; Lloyd Vernon Moore, professor of Bible and religious studies; Florence Peebles, professor of biology; and Carl Salomon, professor of English. Each had a Ph.D., and most possessed years of teaching experience. Peebles, a Bryn Mawr Ph.D. in 1900, had taught for forty-five years. Odell enticed her to move to Portland to help shape the curriculum in biology. Moore earned his Ph.D. from the University of Chicago and was formerly a faculty member at the University of Tulsa. Groening had earned his Ph.D. at Kansas and had taught at Albany College and Linfield. Salomon, a University of Colorado Ph.D., left the University of Idaho to work at Lewis & Clark.

Odell employed a fascinating strategy to build academic standing. He turned to proven professors, distinguished as teachers and scholars but, in several instances, retired from other institutions. He hired Eleanor Ruth Rockwood, head of reference for thirty-five years at the Multnomah County Library, to organize the library in the Albany Quadrangle. John Stark Evans, professor and conductor at the University of Oregon for twenty years, was chosen to develop

music instruction. Norman Coleman, president emeritus of Reed, joined the faculty in 1944 as lecturer in literature as did his wife, Ethel Coleman, in 1946. U. G. Dubach, who earned his Ph.D. at Wisconsin in 1913, came from Oregon State to serve from 1947 to 1958 in political science. Harold Sax Tuttle, who earned his doctorate at Columbia, taught from 1947 to 1956 in education. These older faculty, along with Charles Howard, who came from Whitman in 1944 to serve as dean and professor of psychology until 1958, served as role models for younger faculty and as inspiring teachers for students.

Odell's work in faculty development was integral to turning the institution around. He faced pressures from several directions. The accreditation visit in 1942 from the Northwest Association noted progress but observed fiscal instability and inadequacy of facilities for a fully operating college. The lawn above the swimming pool, for example, failed to qualify as an athletic field. The Oregon State System of Higher Education in 1942 ominously terminated accepting transfer credits from the College. Spirited appeals by Odell and Professor McAfee secured deferral and probationary extension.

One of the most pressing tasks was to dispose of the Monteith Campus in Albany and pay its debts. Efforts of the Albany Chamber of Commerce, College trustees, and Sen. Charles McNary led in 1943 to purchase of the buildings and grounds for $134,500 by the Department of the Interior for use by the Bureau of Mines. The incoming funds only confirmed the College's precarious situation. The trustees paid $132,000 on debts for the facilities and $2,000 to the Albany Chamber of Commerce for expediting the sale. Lewis & Clark College realized $500. The greatest benefit, however, was freedom from responsibility for the Monteith Campus and its debts. With a sense of relief, President Odell reported: "The College is better off financially than it has been in twenty years." The College next secured provisional accrediting, and in 1946 the Northwest Association extended full accreditation.

World War II impacted both the College and the United States. With peace in 1945 a flood of veterans converged on institutions of higher education. Older, traveled, and highly motivated, they wanted an education. To cope with the demand, the College took advantage of war surplus. Crews moved the infirmary from Henry Kaiser's shipyards at Vancouver, Washington, to campus in 1947 to become dining commons, bookstore, and student union. Workmen brought the Officers' Club from Camp Adair near Corvallis to serve as an auditorium and theatre with offices and music practice rooms on its mezzanine. They placed this building at the north end of the campus overlooking the ravine adjacent to the Riverview Cemetery tract. The WAC Training Center at the Portland Air Base became faculty offices and the Department of Business Administration. The library from the Portland Air Base found a perch atop a concrete block foundation and, as Sacajawea Hall, served the Department of Speech Arts. A barracks from Kirkland, Washington, became in 1947 McAfee House, a dormitory for thirty-four men.

While the improvements were temporary and founded on federal financing through the Mead-Lanham Act, the College also sought other solutions to its growth. In 1944 Glen Stanton prepared a campus master plan. Similar to one drawn by Albert Doyle in 1913 for Albany's Monteith Campus, Stanton's plan found inspiration in Thomas Jefferson's layout for the University of Virginia. Stanton envisioned three quadrangles: a faculty residential area with community church on Palatine Hill Road; major buildings, including dormitories, along the formal gardens' main axis; and a classroom

quad extending in a north-south direction on a terrace above Albany. Stanton and Hollis Johnston designed a three-part science complex as the first unit. Although wartime shortages plagued construction, workmen completed it in 1946 to a point that students and faculty moved in for fall semester. The building was named in honor of Charles and Elizabeth BoDine; Elizabeth had served fifteen years on the board and was a founder of the Women's League.

As "Bundles for Britain" encouraged Americans to provide aid to the beleaguered residents of the British Isles, "Bricks for BoDine" became a campus rallying cry in the late 1940s. Carpenters removed temporary plywood panels and installed doors. For weeks President Odell rose at 4:30 A.M. to plug in electric heaters in the classrooms. A hulking boiler from an oil field belched fire and smoke to provide additional heat. Crews finally connected BoDine Hall to the central heating system, and students and faculty raised funds to place brick veneer on the building exterior. Unable to fund Stanton's grand campus plan, the College in 1946 completed grading for the athletic field and began construction of a gymnasium. The basketball team, coached by Eldon Fix, played on plywood because a shortage of maple delayed installation of a hardwood floor.

"The future of a college rests not alone with its campus and buildings, but with its purpose, and the energy, intelligence and spirit with which the college seeks to realize that purpose," wrote Morgan Odell in 1948. The vision grew as students clamored for admission to Lewis & Clark. Courses and new majors met part of that demand. The College also expanded its "Vocational and Special Fields." These included work in home economics, journalism, education, physical education, and business administration. The latter reflected the thriving post-war economy's need for courses in accounting, advertising, business management, merchandising and marketing, personnel, and secretarial training. Dean Charles Howard hired Marjorie Fessenden to teach accounting and Edith Smith to instruct secretarial students in makeshift classrooms in the former garage of the mansion's basement. The College also expanded its pre-professional training in dentistry, medicine, law, engineering, nursing, youth leadership, and the ministry.

The GI Bill of Rights funded many developments. The government paid tuition, books, fees, and a stipend of $75 per month for one year, plus as many additional months as a veteran served in the military. Married veterans received the same benefits plus a living allowance of $105 a month. Public Law 16 expanded benefits to include payments for dependent children while parents attended college. Attendance swelled, surging in 1949 to 1,411.

Lewis & Clark returned to intercollegiate football in 1946 under Coach Robert (Matty) Mathews, former coach at the University of Washington and Notre Dame. Lewis & Clark won three and lost four games that year. Coach Fix's basketball team defeated all except Linfield and took pride in scoring 110 points to Reed's 54. Joe Huston became football coach in 1947 after Mathews' death.

Throughout the 1940s and the 1950s there was no doubt about the Christian character and Presbyterian relationship of the College. Student groups ranging from the Student Christian Association to Inter-Varsity Christian Fellowship, compulsory chapel, weekly Religion-In-Life discussions, and Christian believer clauses in the faculty contracts testified to that commitment. "This is a Christian college," said Odell to Neil Sabin one day in 1949 when he interviewed the prospective speech professor. Odell then asked Sabin about his graduate study at Northwestern University and his role as a military instructor during World War II. Finally Odell turned

◄ Photo of Rod Astor, '54; Dick White, '57; Jim Garrett, '54; Dick Whipple, '53; John Maloney, '53; Bill Jensen, '54; Al Peters, '56; and Phil Dalquist, '52. In 1952, the Delta Tau Rho Model T appeared in the swimming pool, and the mystery was unsolved until 1987 when Pat Hibbard, '52, of Lambda Phi Epsilon fraternity, confessed to the deed. Photo, courtesy of Robert "Bob" Bissell, '54. ▲ The Albany and Portland campus collections—integrated by Eleanor Ruth Rockwood—were housed in the Wallace Howe Lee Library in 1944.

to him and said: "Do you drink?" Thinking the president was going to offer him whiskey, Sabin responded: "No, thank you, it's a little early for me." President Odell sort of gasped, Sabin recalled, and said something about calling him in a couple of weeks. Ultimately Odell made the call and offered Sabin the position.

Music instruction confirmed the vibrant nature of the College in the 1950s. John Stark Evans hired Stanley Glarum to conduct the choir, Boris Sirpo to conduct the orchestra, George Bishop to develop the Madrigal Singers, John Richards to direct the band, and Frances Barry Turrell and Reinhard Pauly to teach musicology. David Campbell, son of the former president of the University of Oregon, had joined the staff in 1948 to teach piano. An attorney by training, a talented organist, and director of the Portland Men's Glee Club, Evans would say to new faculty recruits: "What do you want to teach?" If they responded, "what do you need," he would say: "it is not what I need but what you *want* to do." His strategy created a remarkable program in music.

Each Thursday John Richards left campus to teach clinics and work with high school band teachers. Within a year or so Richards had to put a limit of fifty-four on the College band—he could handle no more. At one time twenty-one of his College students also played in the Oregon Symphony. Glarum, a remarkable choral conductor from Battle Ground, Washington, also went out to public schools. Glarum drew in students, composed and arranged, published, and took his choir on popular West Coast tours. Boris Sirpo, an intense Finn and noted teacher of violin, had a passionate commitment to orchestral music and soon had a full symphony at Lewis & Clark. By the 1950s the College had the sixty-voice College Choir, the Madrigal Singers, a Men's Glee, and a Chapel Choir. Evans was the ultimate conductor, for he took a faculty of soloists and coaxed them into playing to the same tune. He always listened to an idea and would then pose the question: "Now how can we do it?" The College named Evans Hall for him in 1957 at his retirement. Herbert and Ruth Templeton, special friends of music at Lewis & Clark, were principal donors for the $410,000 building.

The upward spiral of enrollment led to the hiring of younger faculty. Donald Balmer recalled, "It seemed that every department had 'an old man and a boy.'" With the Korean War's outbreak and an exodus of students in 1951, the College faced retrenchment. Odell and Howard found a solution: they encouraged the "boys" to complete their doctoral studies in anticipation of renewed enrollments. Several returned to graduate school or finished degrees in progress. Reinhard Pauly headed to Yale; William Stafford, to the University of Iowa; Donald Balmer and Robert Dusenbery, to the University of Washington; Neil Sabin, to Stanford; Arthur Throckmorton, to the University of Minnesota; and John Harrington, to Princeton. These younger faculty earned degrees from major institutions and returned to replace the "old men" and serve the College for decades.

Lewis & Clark held a unique position in the late 1940s and early 1950s. Its tuition was competitive with the state universities in Eugene and Corvallis. Portland State University, then known as Vanport College, initially provided no competition either in programs or price. Possessing limited dormitory rooms, the College operated as a commuter school, and hundreds of students eagerly traveled to and from Palatine Hill. As federal monies and low-interest loans became available, however, the College embarked on new building programs. It erected Akin Hall in 1949 for $210,000 to house sixty-two women, and Stewart Hall in 1951 for $275,000 for ninety-two women and the infirmary.

▲ Herbert Templeton and his wife Ruth played a pivotal role in building the campus physical plant. They gave time, love, resources, and their spirit, embodied in the Templeton College Center dedicatory quote, located in the foyer: "The joy of youth is their delight."

The men slant their long ladders
against the naked building facade,
slapping on paint with measured
abandon . . . It soon takes shape.

Comments on Templeton College Center expansion
Voyageur, 1965

▲ Built in stages, Templeton College Center was dedicated in
1958 to Herbert and Ruth Templeton. A number of rooms are
named after special people in the College's history, including Lewis
Thayer, dean of faculty; U. G. Dubach, political science professor;
the Monteith family; Edward Geary, Elbert Condit, and Wallace
Howe Lee, Albany College presidents; Arthur Fields and Edward
Stamm, trustees; and William Henry Gray, pioneer missionary.

It's a light thing, a bounce, to live here;
the Oregon day crowds in at the door,
say in Templeton, its air cool
and the smell of rain brought all over us
as we smell the fog in its paw,
our breath moving to get loose
in the woods or over the water . . .

PROFESSOR WILLIAM E. STAFFORD
Commencement Address, 1963

▲ David Craig, '90, and Eric Wold, '90, wrote *A Natural History Guide to the Lewis & Clark College Campus*, an assessment of the flora and fauna found on Palatine Hill. They drew on the writings of Benjamin Thaxter, who taught the first field biology classes at Fir Acres. With well over one hundred tree species, the College grounds are among the most botanically diverse in Portland.

Dean Lewis Thayer, a chemist with a doctorate from Stanford who joined the faculty in 1946, served from 1958 to 1969 as dean of faculty. "A quiet voice," his colleagues said of him. In his gentle way Thayer worked through the College's curricular transition from offering basic skills courses to liberal arts, dropping majors and sometimes any instruction in nursing, home economics, secretarial science, personnel, youth leadership, and accounting. By 1964 Lewis & Clark had focused on twenty-one majors. All students studied on the "3-3" plan in three terms of eleven weeks, with about a third of their work in electives, a third in their major, and a third in general requirements. The College prescribed thirty-seven classes for graduation.

Morgan Odell retired in 1960 to the accolades of the many communities he had served. Trustees, Presbyterians, civic officials, political leaders, faculty, students, and alumni praised him as an outstanding educator, a shaper of character, and the man who had helped create Lewis & Clark College. The College named Ruth Odell Hall in 1956 for his wife and willing assistant through eighteen busy years in Portland. To celebrate his contributions an anonymous donor gave a $1,000,000 challenge gift to be matched in five years to expand the College's endowment. Morgan Odell served as a remarkable president whose life and labor bespoke poise under stress, humility in the face of achievement, faith to persevere when the going was tough, and a religious conviction that shone in all he did.

The College leadership passed to an ambitious, articulate man from Illinois. John Howard, age thirty-seven, became one of the nation's youngest college presidents in 1960, when he joined Lewis & Clark. Howard had taught political science at the University of Pennsylvania and served as acting president of Lake Forest College, where he helped restructure the curriculum, implement budget reforms, and strengthen the endowment. The new president faced an enormous assignment. Odell's stature and hold had fixed a pattern difficult for any new administrator to follow or change, yet everywhere were currents portending stormy times. The tempest of national events of the civil rights movement, the assassinations of American leaders, the morass of the Vietnam War, student activism and protest, the spreading use of drugs, and disenchantment with established values and institutions rocked the United States. No college remained isolated, and neither did Lewis & Clark.

By the mid-1960s the College began to stir, assess itself, and test its values. What had seemed certain, became less clear. Where Presbyterian interest had coincided with the College's well-being, now the church examined new ways to expend precious mission dollars. Where classroom instruction had once sufficed, students expressed a hunger to reach beyond the campus to learn life's lessons as well as to meet degree requirements. Old verities—and organizations—came under close scrutiny. Like the Columbus Day Storm which devastated the campus, destroying the Peebles Biology Building in October 1962, forces were building that would transform the institution.

Aeschylus told in *Prometheus Bound* how his fettered hero gave so much for mankind. "And more than all I gave them fire," he said, then added prophetically: "Through it they will learn many arts." The Promethean labors of a dedicated corps of committed people transformed Albany College into a new institution. Lewis & Clark College warmed from the fires they lit, spread across the green hills near Portland, and embarked with vigor to teach many arts.

▲ In 1960, Senator John F. Kennedy, Democratic presidential candidate, made a campaign stop at the College. Over the years, the College has hosted numerous political figures from every persuasion at the local, state, national, and international levels.

May Day bright but we celebrated
in the armory.
Big crowd out to see Marion crowned.
All the dances and other features
of program well given.
Much dishwashing in kitchen
necessitated by big crowd.
Bonfire across the river closes festivities.

Orange Peal, 1917

▲ May Fete began in 1908 and included crowning the queen, a proclamation, music, dance, and winding the Maypole. It continued on the Fir Acres campus until 1967. The 1950 May Fete Court is left to right: Kathleen McGogy, '51; Doreen Donald, '52; Shirley Kanzler, '51; Queen Shirley Bender, '50; Patricia Ambrose, '50; Donna Gaylord, '51; and Nancy Nagues, '53. ▶ From 1946 to 1977, Eldon Fix coached track and cross-country teams to twenty-two Northwest Conference titles. Fix also was alternate coach for 1968 Olympics in Mexico City. Medals are courtesy of Karl Klooster, '62.

◄ Designed by architect Paul Thiry, the chapel was named in honor of generous friend and former trustee Agnes Flanagan. The design drew inspiration from the shape of a Northwest Coast Indian basket hat and the small Manor turret. ▲ In 1967, construction of the chapel sparked controversy from well-dressed protesters. In 1970 Professor John Callahan spoke at an anti-Vietnam War rally.

▲ Dean Sempert's 1963-64 Pioneer basketball team competed in the NAIA tournament. Sempert, '49, led the team to more than 350 wins in twenty-six years. Jim Boutin, '64, NAIA All-American, and Ron Hergert, '65, show enthusiasm after their win over Eastern Oregon. ▶ Coach Joe Huston catapulted the Pioneer football team to success, winning 100 games during his eighteen seasons as coach. The 1950 team capped its undefeated season with a 61-7 victory over San Francisco State. The College playing fields are named in Huston's honor, as is the award for the Athlete of the Year.

In 1947, our football coach,
Matty Matthews died. President Odell
told me to hire a new coach or I would
have to coach the team. I knew Joe Huston
was the top high school coach in Oregon.
I hired him within three days.

PROFESSOR EMERITUS ELDON FIX
at the posthumous induction
of Huston into the Oregon Sports Hall of Fame, 1991

I think about this shy, silent man,
who has never made a fanfare
about his generosity. His life follows
closely the principle that one who does not have to
seek recognition
is really giving from the heart.
His is a gift that is of love and concern.

DR. ROBERT B. PAMPLIN, JR., '64
regarding his father, Robert B. Pamplin, Sr.
Another Virginian, 1986

◄ In 1976, trustee chairman Robert Pamplin, Sr., and President John Howard welcomed President Ford, who spoke on foreign policy in Pamplin Sports Center. ▲ In 1966, the gym on Palatine Hill burned. To build Pamplin Sports Center, honoring the Pamplin family, required $2.2 million. They have aided in development since 1956 through capital campaigns, the endowment, alumni relations, academic chairs, and programs in business administration and economics. Robert Pamplin, Sr., is a life trustee; Robert Pamplin, Jr., is a trustee and was elected board chairman in 1991.

*We face both unparalleled opportunities
and challenges in the coming decades.
Building on the unique heritage
and the strong foundation already established, we
are enthusiastic and excited about this future.*

PRESIDENT JAMES A. GARDNER
"Where Courage Leads," 1987

▲ Opened in 1954, Platt Hall provided housing for 120 male students and social rooms for fraternities. In 1960, the College dedicated an annex named for Charles Howard, dean and vice president, 1944-62. Thoughtful planning provided integration of buildings into the natural forest setting. ▶ In 1981, on the occasion of James Gardner's inauguration as Lewis & Clark's third president, presidents emeriti Morgan Odell, 1942-60, and John Howard, 1960-81, paused for a photo on the steps of the Manor House.

◄ Students visit at the Olin Physics and Chemistry Laboratory Building, situated at the eastern end of the cobblestone drive which runs from the main college entrance. ▼ The bridge to the chapel is named for Wallace Howe Lee who joined the faculty in 1886 and served as president from 1895-1905 and again from 1915-1920. He taught all upper division classes, conferred degrees in Latin, took his salary only after all other salaries and expenses were paid, and donated his extensive personal library to the College. In 1936 the Presbyterian Church honored him for forty-five years as a Presbyterian college educator with its Distinguished Service Award.

▼ In 1954, Professor Ivan Houser, a former student of Gutzon Borglum, sculptor of Mount Rushmore, crafted the Lewis & Clark medallion, a gift of the Class of 1954. The medallion is mounted on a stone block from the Oregonian building, once standing in downtown Portland. ▶ The Forest Hall residence complex.

◄ A trustee since 1942, Rev. Paul Wright, former senior pastor of Portland's First Presbyterian Church, has served the College for more than fifty years as counselor, friend, advocate, theologian-in-residence, and remarkable orator. ▼ The alumni choir performs at the annual holiday service beneath the majestic 4,081 pipe Casavant Freres organ, named for choir director L. Stanley Glarum. The instrument is enhanced by the octagonal design of the chapel.

▼ An aerial view of the College, atop Palatine Hill. The Willamette gently winds past the campus and on through downtown Portland. The Columbia River and Washington State are on the horizon.

Standing by Willamette's waters
Tow'ring o'er its blue
Rises our dear Alma Mater
Proudly to the view.

Where the town and snow-capped mountain
Charm the heart and eye,
There our love will center ever,
Love that cannot die.

Swell the chorus, ever louder
Full of joy and cheer,
Hail to thee, our Alma Mater—
Lewis and Clark, so dear.

▲ "Learning to live with 900 people isn't easy; neither is sharing a bathroom with forty. The need to escape the telephones, stereos, and hair dryers intensifies as time and tolerance wear thin. We are fortunate to have such a myriad of hiding places— from one end of Palatine Road to the other, we are free to explore and escape in beauty and solitude." – *Yiem Kimtah, 1981.*

WIDER HORIZONS

Growth after World War II enabled Lewis & Clark College to embark on exciting explorations. As the forces of history sharpened interest in events far from campus, the College moved in new directions. "All studies in human affairs and in sacred subjects are bound together," wrote Coluccio Salutati in his fourteenth-century *Defense of Liberal Studies*, "and a knowledge of one subject is not possible without a sound and well-rounded education." The College sought a balanced education and to stretch its students. It reached out to the nation and to the world to draw speakers and performers, and presented topical symposia, art exhibits, and fairs.

The College addressed new constituencies. The Law School day program, as well as night classes and work in environmental law, represented new initiatives. The community was served by graduate work in education, educational administration, public administration, counseling psychology, and special education for the hearing-impaired. The College also developed ancillary entities: the Institute for Study of American Language and Culture, Northwest Writing Institute, and a Continuing Education Division offering weekend classes, conferences, and special workshops. Summer offerings included courses in all majors.

This drew on new resources, expanded program impact, dictated construction, and challenged administrators, faculty, and staff. "Let a certain holy ambition invade our souls," wrote Giovanni Pico della Mirandola in 1486, "so that, not content with the mediocre, we shall pant after the highest and (since we may if we wish) toil with all our strength to obtain it." "Holy ambition" echoed through the College and led to efforts in the 1980s to sharpen focus and define roles. Some worked; but others plunged the campus into debate. The College survived. It proved larger than issues, individuals or differences. It was an integrating factor in society and an investment of creativity, energy, and resources, honoring its roots in Renaissance humanism and the classics, yet expanding its horizons.

"What *is* important is the opportunity to learn from a faculty alert to the dynamic world about them and eager to share with students their insight into the implications of the changes which are constantly occurring," noted the *Catalog* in 1963-64. Commitment to the "3-3" plan fixed general studies, electives, and the major which became the pattern for generations of students. President John Howard began this plan, hoping to bond the institution through shared reading and discussion. "Reading Week" in 1963 initiated the process with the topic of "The Individual in America." Students and faculty read Henry Thoreau's *Walden*, William Douglas's *America Challenged*, and Ayn Rand's *Atlas Shrugged*, and gathered for several days of lectures, films, and discussion.

Supreme Court Justice Douglas and Ayn Rand, a proponent of "objectivism," presented lectures. Rand's speaking sparked such interest that her visit became a reference point in the school's history. Rand rose during the showing of "The Fountainhead," a film based on her novel, and screamed the projector to silence. With four-letter expletives, she gave a resounding denunciation of "collectivists and liberals" who, she alleged, had cut the pivotal speeches of her heroine and hero. Rand declared: "This is an example of what I've been fighting all my life. They'll stop at nothing to keep

◄ *Students on Alvord Desert, southeastern Oregon.* ▲ *Graduates wear colors of the flags of countries they are from or where they have studied.*

my views from the public." An honorary degree of doctor of humane letters, the only such degree Rand ever received, fueled more controversy and shaped faculty resolve to exert more control over Reading Week.

In winter term the faculty promoted "Contemporary Threats to Individualism" and recommended Eric Hoffer's *The True Believer* and David Riesman's *The Lonely Crowd*. Hoffer captured the community with his homespun wit. Philosopher Sidney Hook lectured in spring, emphasizing "Individual Responsibility in the Corporate World." Unlike the first Reading Week, however, the students faced classes to discuss Hook's writings and J. D. Salinger's *Nine Short Stories*. Reading Week sputtered, then died, but its impact remained. The speakers energized a college and set a new tone.

A mirror to the College's new face arose in the 1960s in faculty discussions of the meaning of academic excellence. "Our aim is not to show the student what to think but how to think," stated John Harrington, professor of philosophy. Eugene Kozloff, professor of biology, argued that the College should nurture rigorous work in a specific field. "You cannot build an intellectual climate," he noted, "if 50 percent of the students are learning a trade." "A known faculty," stressed Donald Balmer, professor of political science, "is the most important factor for the college to become academically known."

The faculty demonstrated their commitment to the life of the mind. Bernard Hinshaw's paintings, Norman Paasche's calligraphy, and Ken Shores's ceramics gained selection in shows. Historian Joachim Remak published *Sarajevo* (1960) and *The Gentle Critic: Theodor Fontane and German Politics, 1848-1868* (1964); Arthur Throckmorton wrote *Argonauts on the Oregon Frontier* (1961); and Robert Cruden wrote *James Ford Rhodes: The Man, the Historian and His Work* (1961) and *The Negro in Reconstruction* (1969). William Stafford penned poetry and essays and won the National Book Award for poetry in 1962 for *Traveling Through the Dark;* his stature took him across the country to speak, read, and serve as poetry consultant to the Library of Congress. Vern Rutsala's poetry appeared in the *Paris Review, Epoch,* and *The Nation* and became *The Window* (1964). Stanley Glarum continued production of choral compositions and arrangements; Boris Sirpo took his orchestral groups on tour; Edith Kilbuck won the Petri Award and gained a national reputation as a harpsichordist; and Reinhard Pauly wrote *Music in the Classic Period* (1965), *Music and Theater* (1967), and contributed to the *New Grove Dictionary of Music and Musicians*. The faculty confirmed through these activities and participation in their professional organizations that they, too, were students. Their commitment to read, reflect, write, and perform became part of the tenure and performance review adopted in the 1970s.

Change also came in the relationship between the Presbyterian Church and the College. The ties had endured for nearly a century and had repeatedly helped sustain Albany College and Lewis & Clark College. But in the 1960s America sharpened the separation between church and state. Congress funded higher education in an effort to gain an edge in the exploration of space and in technology. The money dangled with strings attached. Lewis & Clark College had to unravel its bond with the Synod of Oregon to qualify for federal dollars. The need for government grants and loans for the various construction projects required by a growing college pressed heavily. Thus in 1966 the trustees and the Synod jointly agreed to sever the bonds which had served mutual interest. Henceforth Lewis & Clark College was an independent, liberal arts college which affirmed its historic ties with the Presbyterians. Its

Board of Trustees held full responsibility for the assets, direction, governance, and staffing.

The dissolution of ties with the Synod alarmed some and pleased others—and led to changes. The College dropped religion course requirements and compulsory chapel. The position of chaplain remained and even grew: in 1974 Rev. Paul Wright, retired pastor of Portland's First Presbyterian Church, became theologian in residence. Speaking with what some insisted was the "voice of God," he was a gentle counselor. He advised faculty, married students, quoted great writers, and served as a link with the past.

In the 1960s and 1970s engagement in social issues captured the attention of the College. Forces in society shook complacency and insularity, tested administrative skills, tugged at students and faculty, and led to comparison with other schools. Was the College too conservative? Was it too liberal? Could it walk the line between inquiry into controversial ideas, yet draw on the philanthropy of conservatives? These were years of tension. When they passed, Lewis & Clark was a different place: The May Fete was no more; Greek organizations nearly disappeared as did the Erodelphians, Amicans, Sacajaweans, Blue Key, and Gold Key; and Otto Sack Day was forgotten. What was relevant to one era was irrelevant to another. Such was the pace of history.

The tide came inexorably. The civil rights movement began it, and the campus reflected the impact of instantaneous news coverage. Students saw televised freedom marches, sit-ins, and attempts by blacks to enter state-supported schools in the South. Violence, shootings, suppression of protest with fire hoses and police dogs, and national outrage found audience on campus.

The "Statement of Purpose" in the 1964 *Catalog* affirmed that "Lewis and Clark is concerned to prepare students to take responsible and creative positions in a world of constant change, increasing interdependence and rapidly expanding knowledge. . . ." Those words took on meaning as news events, films, readings, discussions, and speakers on various issues plunged the campus into awareness and debate. In 1962, student leaders wrote a letter admonishing the University of Mississippi for "intolerable and unconstitutional actions toward those of other races." James Meredith's enrollment in that institution had reverberated across the United States. Roy Wilkins, national director of the NAACP, addressed the freshman convocation in 1964. Within a month, under President Howard and his assistant, Freeda Hartzfeld, students began a "One-on-One" tutoring program, assisting inner-city children in Portland's public schools. The persistence of student commitment to this service meshed well the following year with Reading Week's selection of C. Vann Woodward's *The Strange Career of Jim Crow* and Howard Zinn's *The New Abolitionists*. The opportunity to hear these men speak confirmed the determination to face issues of civil rights.

Large audiences attended lectures by Whitney Young, executive director of the National Urban League and Rev. Martin Luther King, Jr., of the Southern Christian Leadership Alliance; and questions and answers about apartheid with John B. Mills, consul general for South Africa. Articles in the *Log* by Professor Arleigh Dodson and student Bill Hayden about their experiences in voter registration in 1964 in Mississippi gave immediacy to issues.

Nothing cut so deep, however, as the Vietnam War. The nation's polarization was mirrored on campus as students, faculty, and administrators struggled with the issues, ongoing programs, free inquiry, and the boundaries of advocacy. William Stafford, John Crist, Hideo Hashimoto, and Robert Martin took a public position

Education must be for a world of change,
a world yearning
for international interdependence . . .

PRESIDENT JOHN R. HOWARD
Address to Portland Rotary Club, 1961

▲ In 1962, Lewis & Clark College sponsored its first four overseas programs, including the two groups pictured that went to Japan. Led by professors Hideo Hashimoto and Kenneth Johnson, the Japan trip sailed from San Francisco on the S.S. *President Cleveland*.

▲ Overseas programs involve study of geographical areas, language, culture, and independent study. *Above left:* Michell Courkamp, '80; Megs Muldrow, '81; Wil Lum, '80; Brigit Binns, '79; and Mark Benson, '81, visited a Buddhist shrine in Hong Kong. The trip was led by history professor Jeffrey Barlow. *Above right:* the 1968-69 Austria group, led by physics professor Robert Martin, explored a salt mine. *Below right:* Robert Jenkins, '84, joined other students and leader Del Smith and his wife Helen, for six months in Kenya.

in 1965 when they questioned rights under the Selective Service Act. As conscientious objectors and war opponents, they wanted students to be aware of options. The campus Young Democrats acted, too. Ken Bowden, its president, said: "The lack of interest at Lewis and Clark makes it better for us to affiliate with SDS than try to compete with them." The turn toward Students for a Democratic Society confirmed that some students embraced a more activist role in political affairs. A few months later Professor Karlin Capper-Johnson moderated a debate on the war in Vietnam: President Howard took the pro-American involvement position and Professor William Lewis advocated getting out of Vietnam.

Tension mounted in 1966. Protesters picketed Vice President Hubert Humphrey. Others denounced a sign at the library for crediting President Lyndon Johnson. "Beware the day when LBJ receives recognition in red, white and blue for constructing a library of which he knows nothing and cares less," read the *Log*. In 1967 an anti-Vietnam group formed, and protesters surrounded Marine Corps recruiters. "There comes a time when in spite of all the frustrations you feel, you must say, 'I don't know what I can do, but here I must stand,'" said Gordon Verplank, campus chaplain. Five weeks later students held Vietnam Day.

Campus events of 1968 echoed—from denunciation of American involvement in Vietnam by Brig. Gen. Tran Van Dinh to ideological confrontation between the themes of May Fete and Reading Week. Civil rights activists Howard Fuller and Tom Hayden came to campus to lecture in the program, "Sounds of the Black Ghetto—A Powerless Community." They found May Fete preparations under way with the theme "Tara." "You whites dream of Tara-like mansions drenched with southern colonial atmosphere," thundered Fuller. "Near Duke University, North Carolina's Harvard of the South, blacks spend their lives in shabby termite-infested shacks that might have belonged to slaves. Can't you find the quaint southern atmosphere there?" Within days the Black Student Union issued demands, and the United Student Front presented ten ultimatums. The BSU and USF wanted commitment to minority enrollment and hiring a black professor. The USF called for longer library hours, a stop to job recruiting by war-related industries, and termination of questions about drug use or psychiatric care in selection of students to study overseas. They called for a stop to complying with the Selective Service until recision of General Hershey's order to classify student demonstrators 1A, subject to immediate draft.

The *Log* heralded 1968 as "The Year of Action." Events confirmed that assessment. The Students Organized for Social Action invited an array of entertainers and speakers. The Free University with classes on "The Effects of Marijuana," "Stereo Equipment," "Mao's Guerilla Warfare," and "Communal Living" drew several hundred. Resident advisors pressed for student control of inter-visitation in dormitories. The heated atmosphere of May 1968 also stemmed from the Oregon primary where Richard Nixon, Ronald Reagan, Nelson Rockefeller, Eugene McCarthy, and Robert Kennedy all sought votes in their bids for the presidency.

The times tried the patience and values of the campus community. In 1969 an enraged faculty member called in the FBI to arrest a student he alleged was illegally wearing a navy officer uniform. The issue divided the faculty and led the administration to intercede, with assistance from the Law School, to gain dismissal of the charges. In 1970 David Poulschock and Rand Dawson joined three hundred other students in the White House "To Seek Answers Together." Poulschock met Nixon and reported: "There was no

togetherness and there were no answers." Opposition to the war led Professors John Brown and John Hart to bring before the faculty a resolution, passed unanimously, to suspend classes and observe on October 15 a national moratorium to discuss peace and war. More than six hundred gathered, including John Crampton of the political science department, who said, "One loves one's country not for what it is, but what it ought to be—one says this over and over."

When President Nixon ordered troops into Cambodia in 1970, the ASLC called for a student strike. The killing of students on Kent State's campus, the raising of the American flag (upside down) to half-mast on campus, the dismissal of some classes, the efforts of President Howard to keep the campus operating, and the cry of a female student "At what price?" to his remarks—all were seared into memory as vividly as the Columbus Day Storm and Kennedy's assassination. Before the week was out ASLC president Poulschock resigned; Howard refused to authorize a referendum on Vietnam; and faculty and students proceeded to vote on the issues.

Lewis & Clark's horizons expanded. Speakers came from many lands and persuasions. W. H. Auden, distinguished British poet, drew more than two thousand in 1967. Eli Weisel, Dick Gregory, Tony Miranda, Paul Ehrlich, and Robert Redford lifted up social and environmental issues. John F. Kennedy, Wayne Morse, Eugene McCarthy, Robert Packwood, Mark Hatfield, Gerald Ford, and others sought votes or explained policy. Anais Nin, writer; Martha Graham, dancer and choreographer; Agnes Moorehead, actress; the San Francisco Mime Troupe; pipe organist Virgil Fox; and harpsichordist Ralph Kirkpatrick—all enriched the College.

Founded in 1964, the Throckmorton Lecture Series included historians Carl Degler, Henry Steele Commager, Kenneth Stampp, Gerda Lerner, John Hicks, and Carolyn Lougee. Convocation speakers included John Glubb Pasha, Richard Leakey, and Ben Bradley, and annual Religion-in-Life theologians. Where it had drawn on West Coast educators and Presbyterian ministers for graduation remarks, now the College turned to national figures.

Awareness grew with the founding in 1965 of the Ethics and International Affairs Symposium. Professor Karlin Capper-Johnson, devoted to student engagement in issues through Model United Nations conferences, set the tone for the first gathering, which brought speakers from India, Vietnam, and New Zealand. These events exposed the campus to pressing issues, major figures, and diverse perspectives. One symposium brought Edwin Reichauer, Hans Morganthau, Robert Scalapino, and the Soviet consul general to campus. Professor Joseph Ha drew upon his acquaintances in Asia, the Soviet Union and the State Department as speakers.

Not all efforts to stretch the community continued. In 1971 the College hosted the Spiritual Quest Symposium. A "swami," a psychic, a researcher in parapsychology, and a man identified only as "Louis" talked about auras, astral projection, clairvoyance, love, precognition, and reincarnation. It was not repeated. The First (and last) International Conference on the Writings of Immanuel Velikovsky drew crowds and faculty skepticism. But the 1970 symposium, "Women's Liberation and Men's Freedom," featuring Sally Linton and Gloria Steinem presaged the Gender Studies Symposium, begun in 1982. That series elicited student and faculty papers, drew feminists and writers in gender studies, and explored subjects from sexuality to pronouns.

Civil rights and war and peace issues informed social consciences in the 1960s, but environmental issues began to gain interest. In 1969, the biology and physics departments offered a new course,

Environmental Crisis. Donald Balmer, political science professor, taught Resource Issues. Students held Earth Day in 1970 and recycled beverage containers. John Piacentini, '52, owner of the Plaid Pantry, offered refunds for bottles prior to Oregon's Bottle Bill. These events led to student-designed majors in environmental studies and an internship program which placed students in career-related opportunities in the Portland area.

Interest in the environment, social justice, peace, war, and international relations meshed with the College's growing commitment to overseas and off-campus study. That program's origins stemmed from diverse factors. President John Howard, an ardent traveler, and several trustees and friends of the College talked about "cultural interdependence." They envisioned young people meeting different societies head-on through living with host families, studying a new language, exploring a foreign land, and working in independent studies to learn history, art, literature, or other subjects in a new place. This coincided in 1962 with the "War Baby" boom and oversubscribed dormitories. Part of the overseas program's lure was need for a place for 110 students. The solution was to dispatch twenty to Chile with Ivan Houser, twenty-three to Peru with Clifford Hamar, twenty-four to Mexico with Nosratollah Rassekh, and forty-three to Japan with Hideo Hashimoto and Kenneth Johnson.

This launched an adventure in education which touched thousands of lives. Kathy Becker, living with a family in Hyogo, Japan, wrote in 1962: "We have a Shinto shrine in the living room (which at first I blush to confess I thought was a cuckoo clock) and a Buddhist one in the traditional room." Terry Supahan, a member of the Karuk Tribe and participant in the 1980 program in Israel, wrote how his studies with Professor Richard Rohrbaugh had shaped his life:

> I could never quite shake my feeling that my college experience was surreal. . . . Traveling to Israel in my junior year helped to mitigate my ambivalence towards the college. The trip made my college or academic experience 'real' or relevant to my other life, my home life. It re-energized my studies, and it strengthened my commitment and understanding of scholarship. . . . If I was to return home and try to stake a career on working with my people and my tribe, then I was going to have to squeeze the most out of my liberal arts education and design my own curriculum.

The overseas study program transformed the College. A half-dozen faculty members annually changed routine and grew in perspective. Students returned more mature, determined, and socially aware. The program stimulated related developments. The political science department inaugurated its Washington, D.C., program in 1965. The biology department launched a field biology program in 1968 and helped staff the course, "On the Trail of Lewis and Clark." This offering in botany and ethnohistory won national recognition for following the explorers' footsteps. The departments of art and theatre in 1972 developed one term of study in New York.

These programs generated unique bonds, uniting participants for a lifetime. They tied students to host family, professor, and country. On the train between Khabarovsk and Irkutsk in 1989, John Pearce wrote of a scene: "I stand by an open door behind the kitchen of the train. The wind pounds my face, sending tears down my cheeks. The moving air and bright sun make the land we are passing through all the more beautiful. . . . I contemplate jumping from the train as we begin to slow for a long turn. What would I see if I were to start walking out into this vastness?" The answer rests in the imaginations of those whose lives were changed by the College during the last four decades of the twentieth century.

After 1960, the College's wider horizons were shaped not only by contemporary events, speakers, faculty commitments, symposia, and overseas and off-campus studies, but also by the administration. Presidents, deans, program directors, personnel in student services, and others were committed to innovation, assessment, and refinement. Complacency was not in their vocabulary. While leadership from the Manor House often tested the faculty, it provoked new thinking, curricular changes, and programs.

John Brown left the classroom in 1971 to serve as dean of faculty. He highlighted the faculty in *Catalog* profiles which discussed their teaching philosophy and work. Brown served during the shift from prescribed general requirements to more student choice in the human experience. The Freshman Seminar and, later, Society and Culture, emerged as initiatives with emphasis on critical thinking and writing. In 1985 Basic Inquiry was adopted, in which small classes for all first-year students shared a common curriculum.

In 1963 the State Department began funding a program at Lewis & Clark for language and cultural orientation to foreign students. Commitment to international students grew through the Institute for the Study of American Language and Culture, which often enrolled more than a hundred students for up to two years in a non-degree program. The College developed the Northwest Writing Institute in 1986, directed by Kim Stafford, for classes in writing and to administer the Oregon Folk Arts Program. Non-degree students were also served through Continuing Professional Education. Offerings ranged from sailing to Saturday skill-building workshops—such as those taught by the Indian carver Lelooska—and special workshops in discipline, critical thinking, and music education.

Between 1962 and 1965 the College considered merger with Northwestern College of Law. Clifford Hamar chaired the study committee, and on September 10, 1965, the trustees ratified the merger and named the new graduate unit Northwestern School of Law. Challenges were many, for accreditation by the American Bar Association hinged on funding. The law program moved to Palatine Hill in 1967 and offered evening courses. Development mounted rapidly in 1968 when the Hill Family Foundation granted $125,000 to endow teaching in commercial law and the College embarked on a $2,000,000 campaign to erect buildings, designed by Paul Thiry, for the twenty-acre campus at Boones Ferry Road and Terwilliger Boulevard. In 1970 the College dedicated these facilities and began publication of *Environmental Law*. The first issue included articles by Mark Hatfield, Edmund Muskie, and Richard Nixon. The journal was an important vehicle for sharpening the skills of student editors and drew attention to the law school through publishing work of major figures addressing environmental issues.

The law school secured accreditation and grew by 1980 to the largest law school program in the Pacific Northwest. Dozens of alumni, grateful for the evening programs, helped build facilities to house the law faculty and students. The contributions of time and resources of William Swindells, Sr., Paul Boley, and Gen. Chester McCarty were pivotal. These men saw the need to attract a strong faculty, build up a library, erect a physical plant, and encourage students to study law. Their vision and that of hundreds of others helped propel the law school to national distinction.

*This September, for the first time
at Lewis & Clark, there were more students taking
first year Japanese and Russian
than first year French and German.*

PROFESSOR DINAH DODDS
Foreign Languages Department alumni newsletter, 1988

▲ Students on the 1989-90 trip to Japan enjoy the Noboribetsu onzen. Left to right, Shannon Larsen, '91; Kimberly Carlson, '90; Jean Kim, '90; Lisa Hutchins, '91; and Kirsten Cramer, '91. Besides a flourishing overseas study program led by Lewis & Clark faculty, the College has sister school relationships with Hokusei Gakuen College, Sapporo, Japan; Guangxi Teacher's University in Guilin, the People's Republic of China; Khabarovsk Pedagogical Institute, USSR; and Kyoto University of Foreign Studies, Kyoto, Japan.

Graduate programs also expanded. From work in 1948 for the master of education degree, new degrees and certifications were added. These included master of arts degrees in teaching, public administration, music, and music education; and certificates in education administration, special education for the hearing impaired, and counseling psychology. In 1984 these programs were put under the administration of the Graduate School of Professional Studies. These courses attracted older students. The Graduate School also mounted special seminars. Since 1978, it has staffed the U.S. Forest Service "Intensive Semester," which brings federal land managers to the campus for educational renewal.

John Howard retired in 1981 after twenty-one years as president. He left a remarkable legacy: he led and persuaded others to follow, dreamed of what might be and obtained resources, hired teachers with scholarly interests, and oversaw construction of a new physical plant. That legacy included two libraries, an indoor swimming pool and sports complex, classroom and office buildings, a chapel, and new dormitories. He presided with grace in times of turmoil and left an institution which looked far beyond Palatine Hill.

James Gardner, a graduate of Yale and Harvard, an attorney, and a former official of the Ford Foundation in Brazil became the next president. Confronting Gardner were myriad concerns, including resource allocations and the roles of the undergraduate college, Northwestern School of Law, and the graduate programs. The quest for proper balance raised issues of governance which soon tested the president, trustees, faculty, student body and alumni. The 1980s were a troubled era, as evidenced by the high turnover of administrative staff and deans and in stressful situations that challenged the trustees. Quick resolution proved elusive.

James Gardner was singularly dedicated. Even when faculty members were adversaries, he refrained from criticism. Instead he worked with determination to build the endowment and encourage development of alumni chapters throughout the country, a growth from three to eighteen. When he arrived, the endowment stood at $9.8 million; when he left in 1989, it had reached $24.1 million with additional sums in deferred gifts and bequests as a future legacy. Gardner pressed his staff, led by Gene Gregory, vice president for institutional advancement, to field grant proposals, find friends, and help the endowment grow. In that he succeeded well.

The spirit of liberal studies—the breath of the humanists of the Renaissance—surfaced in a broadening view and "holy ambition." Students met life head-on in courses and in experiences far from campus. Shakers and makers, artists and performers, charlatans and ideologues—all offered their wares. The fifteenth-century advice of François Rabelais, written by Gargantua to his son Pantagruel, resounded in what was taking place:

> *As for a knowledge of the facts of nature, I would have you apply yourself to this study with such curiosity that there should be no sea, river, or stream of which you do not know the fish; you should likewise be familiar with all the birds of the air, all the trees, shrubs, and thickets of the forest, all the grasses of the earth, all the metals hidden in the bellies of the abysses, and the precious stones of all the East and South: let nothing be unknown to you.*

Therein lay the bywords of the College's wider horizons— "let nothing be unknown to you."

▲ Put on by the International Student Association, the International Fair features native costumes, foods, music, and entertainment indigenous to student homelands. Bita Farzanpay, '93, is from Iran.

▲ Foreign students, though few in Lewis & Clark's early years, now represent nearly fifty countries and comprise more than 10 percent of the student body. *Above left:* Stanford Muigai Njuguna, '91, is from Kenya. *Above right:* Fredrik Granstrom, '93, is from Sweden.

RHYTHMS OF COLLEGE LIFE

There are natural rhythms: the thrusting up and wearing down of mountains, the cycle of seasons, growth from infancy to old age, migration of birds, and the cadence of the tides. So, too, is there a pattern to the college year. No matter what decade or which student generation, the course seems as constant as spring following winter or the sun warming the land after rain. The writer of Ecclesiastes eloquently captured this sense of succession and its fit with the human experience:

> To every thing there is a season,
> and a time to every purpose under the heaven:
>   A time to be born, and a time to die;
> a time to plant, and a time to pluck up that which is planted;
>   A time to kill, and a time to heal;
> a time to break down, and a time to build up;
>   A time to weep, and a time to laugh;
> a time to mourn, and a time to dance;
>   A time to cast away stones, and a time to gather stones together;
> a time to embrace, and a time to refrain from embracing;
>   A time to get, and a time to lose;
> a time to keep, and a time to cast away;
>   A time to rend, and a time to sew;
> a time to keep silence, and a time to speak;
>   A time to love, and a time to hate;
> a time of war, and a time of peace.

College years flow with the seasons. At times they are the moments of casting away, building up, getting, living, and finding love and peace. They represent the freshness of youth, definition of being, seizing of responsibility, and joy of discovery. They are a time to dance, to laugh, to speak, and to celebrate the life of the mind. The magic of those years becomes a thread binding together people of different backgrounds, races, philosophies, and generations. The rhythm is inexorable. All who have shared in the life of the College have walked part of the same path.

Michael Mooney was inaugurated president of Lewis & Clark College in 1990. A former deputy provost of Columbia University, Mooney came to Palatine Hill with clear conviction about the value of the liberal arts education in American life. The events surrounding the public ceremony acknowledging his service to the College included lectures by Yasuhiro Nakasone, former prime minister of Japan; a scholars' colloquium, Six Views on Endings and Beginnings; the address of John Brooks Slaughter, a physicist and president of Occidental College; performances of the gamelan opera *The King of Bali;* musical events and an art show.

President Mooney referred to the college experience as "a kind of halfway house between the prison of youth and the liberty of adulthood." In that phrase he captured the tension which for 125 Septembers has gripped College-bound young people. Beginning as a freshman, or "rook," has a bewildering quality. Parents hover, upperclass students lurk, advisers cope with questions, and new students fidget with anxiety. And well they should, for they face placement tests in mathematics and foreign languages, meetings

◄ Women's eight shell practices on the Willamette River. ▲ More than 20,000 graduates of the College have worn the mortarboard and tassel.

with advisers, and simple things—mealtimes, laundry, photo identi-
fication cards, bus schedules, and finding where everything is.

Each new student encounters dislocation; each has to cope with
leaving the familiar and meeting things new. Cindy Greene in
October 1977 captured the feeling when she wrote:

> *Behind me, barely visible through the morning's glare, lay the*
> *hill I'd lived on most of my life. As I adjusted my seat belt, somehow*
> *it seemed that I had really felt more secure in the nervous anxiety of*
> *not knowing where I would go to school—when days were spent*
> *endlessly leafing through college catalogs and guides to college*
> *catalogs—than in the reality of arranging my belongings on the*
> *plane knowing the decision was over and I was definitely going.*

The College tries to ease the beginning. It brings freshmen to
campus a few days before returning students flood to Palatine Hill.
The effort is to give those who are new a modest edge. It also
mounts a campaign, not always successful, to separate parents from
their child. Parents' Preview features discussions by faculty on
course offerings, the value of general education, and—so it seems—
assurance that the cost is worth the investment. For a few hours
freshmen are spared the humiliation of having anyone actually see
their parents, let alone having to listen—yet again—to more advice
on how to avoid red socks, put up with a roommate, or the need to
keep a toothbrush. Finally the ordeal is over. Moms and dads,
younger brothers and sisters, sometimes even a grandparent, say
farewell. New Student Orientation begins as freshmen and transfer
students are caught up in a whirl of activity. The door from the
prison of youth opens wide. Discovery is at hand.

From the 1940s into the 1970s new students suffered modest
indignities. Part of college life was an exercise in enduring hazing:
men wore orange beanies with a black bill; women wore orange
ribbons. Upperclass students expected freshmen to show respect
and perform community labors such as cleaning the reflecting pool.
All this culminated in Rook Week, which pitted freshmen against
sophomores in a tug-of-war or pushball competition. Then came the
kangaroo court with charges against rooks of making Tarzan-like
yells near the dormitories, lacking school spirit, hustling upperclass
students, or failing to wear the obligatory beanies and ribbons. The
penalty was a dunking in the reflecting pool or the outdoor swimming pool. These rites even befell freshmen on overseas trips.
Bound for Japan by ship in 1962, upperclass students produced
black and orange cloth and instructed the rooks to make beanies,
bibs, and ribbons. The ship's pool was the dunk-tank-at-sea.

The opening of the school year has its rituals: convocations,
academic processions, and speakers. It is a time of setting a tone. It
also brings reality: registration, paying bills, shopping in the bookstore, classes, weighing the syllabus (and course requirements), and
campus meal service. The College has tried many ways to facilitate
fitting students into courses and distributing classes by competency
and contractual responsibility of the professors. From punch cards
in 1962 to the computer terminals set up to record student class
choices by the 1970s, the registrar's office stretched to meet this
challenge. Registrar Robert Wilkin presided over this process for
twenty-six years under the slogan "the smaller the line, the better
the registration." Adoption of alphabetical systems for registration
and shifting those over three terms helped in this process.

Freedom and responsibility resound through the opening days of
college. They bear heaviest on the freshmen but impinge on

▲ The Student Activities Fair is a marketplace of organizations and
clubs. With more than fifty active clubs as well as student media,
governance boards, and other opportunities for involvement in
Portland, students learn to balance curricular and co-curricular life.

We were standing on the Berlin Wall,
dancing, singing, turning cart-wheels,
and crying . . . until we realized
we had to get back down somehow.

LAURA MUNDT, '91
of 1990 overseas trip to East/West Germany
"Insider's Guide '91"

▲ "My fears have slipped away to little more than wonder and curiosity of a new home whose first ornament was a memory put on a shelf." – Cindy Greene, 1977, in *Convergence*. Pictured above is Laurie Matthews, '92, in Armstrong Lounge, the Manor House.

Is there a happy medium somewhere
between isolation and claustrophobia,
freedom and dependence?
I think it got lost in the storage room
of my dorm with my bean bag chair
and box of books from last term.

Yiem Kimtah, 1981.

▲ Students traverse the campus grounds between the residence
areas and the classrooms, passing the senior benches, which were
brought to the Portland Fir Acres campus from Albany College.

students as well. Jennie Huntley, a sophomore in 1983, wrote of the maturation taking place in her life:

In the Lewis & Clark experience, independence is often equated with individuality. As a student learns to cope with independence, a unique identity is built upon the layers of experience. Development of this identity is sometimes traumatic, heartrending realizations—when the collect calls home start to increase. Often people have the extreme loneliness of having no one to depend upon. But when Mom and Dad aren't there to fall back on, and the hometown honey can't cut the mustard anymore, we need to fall back on ourselves.

The tapping of inner resources happens fast. There comes the moment of truth that each must master fate. This responsibility goes with freedom.

September is Oregon's kindest month. Days are warm and the air is clear. Rain is only a memory of something that happened months ago. Sun filters through stands of Douglas firs in the ravines, lights the forest floor, sparkles on the pools, and—at sunset—illuminates the tip of Mount Hood. Labor comes early for the crew teams rowing their shells at River Place on the Willamette. Cross-country runners circle the cemetery and the campus, testing endurance. Football players grunt, gasp, slap hands, wheel, turn, and slam together in scrimmages at Griswold Stadium, while soccer players practice at Huston field on Boones Ferry Road. The thud of tennis balls and the thump from squash courts hint at sweaty competition. For five years a Swedish jogging trail encircled the campus, its winding paths and exercise stations—now mostly lost in tangles of ivy—luring runners on a self-paced journey. Late in the day students take the trail toward the river to sail on the Willamette. In the dark the blare of the rock music, clank of free weights, and metallic din of the Universals float from Pamplin's weight room.

Fall term is a time of exploration. Over the years the outdoor programs—Trodse, Trekenspielers, Alpine Club, Ski Club, and now College Outdoors—existed for adventure. Some entering students created their first friendships rafting the Deschutes, climbing Mount St. Helens, or hiking in the Gorge. For others adventure was in Portland: the Saturday Market, the Art Museum, shopping at Nordstrom or Meier & Frank, drinking coffee at Papa Haydn's, shopping at Powell's Bookstore, or examining life at Darcelle XV. There are places to eat: Huber's, Spaghetti Factory, Dan and Louis' Oyster Bar, Salty's, the Crab Bowl, pizza and pancakes. There are watering holes: the Buffalo Gap, Open Seas, Hillsdale Pub, and Billy Bangs. And to meet most needs there was and is Freddy's at Burlingame. The problem for freshmen was—and remains—getting there without an hour's walk, though the ASLC shuttle has helped.

The first week of classes sets the pace. The nimble press to get on the list and off the overload sheet. The timid drop the first day the professor asks for a research paper proposal to be followed in two weeks by a bibliography. The scientific work afternoons in labs where they breathe aromas of formaldehyde and trace the plastic veins and arteries of a cat's circulatory system, a dogtooth shark's anatomy, or a frog's nervous system. Musicians settle in to lessons, practice, and rehearsals, while art students dust off a corner in Peebles to paint, sculpt, or throw a pot. The campus has many niches; part of the first days of school is finding ones that fit.

Learning comes fast, but the lessons are sometimes difficult. How long can I go without doing laundry? Could I mail it home and get it back ironed? Is there a grocery store at Burlingame? How can I sneak in to eat at Fields? Is it worth it if they are serving hamburger-carrot-soybean loaf again? How can I get involved on campus? Does the bookstore take plastic? What is a checking account and how do I balance it? How much can I drink and not get sick? These become life's questions and challenges. They confirm that education goes on beyond the classroom, laboratory, or library. They are part of living, and that, of course, is ultimately what college is about.

The College has attempted to meet student questions and needs through the student affairs staff. In the early years on Palatine Hill the job fell to deans of men and women and resident house mothers. Hester Turner in 1961 became the first woman dean of students. Kent Hawley succeeded Turner and served during the years of student activism and the press for control over living situations and a voice in curriculum and governance. Richard Sorensen became dean of students in 1976. In that role, Sorensen pursued a philosophy of empowering students to make decisions affecting their lives. He hired experienced staff who were willing to reinforce student self-governance, expanded counseling services and the roles of resident directors and resident assistants, increased the range of student activities, and encouraged the admissions staff to continue to broaden the geographical and demographic makeup of the student body.

Often unheralded but critical to new student orientation and the functioning of the College are the support staff: secretaries, grounds crew, maintenance, and security. They answer questions, direct the lost, attend to details, supervise students in work-study programs, and help build a sense of community. Secretaries cope with late papers, missed exams, misunderstandings between students and professors, registration problems, and scheduling. They monitor budgets, remember office hours, and even bring cut flowers to brighten the day.

Fall term is also football season. The sport resumed at the College in 1946 after eight years when the shift to the downtown Portland campus, low enrollments, and World War II precluded putting together a team. Coaches Huston, Wilson, and Smythe fielded teams which have competed in NAIA district and regional playoffs. The Pioneers have had moments of glory: the resounding victories of 1950 and winning in the Pear Bowl and more good years in the 1960s. Newer fall programs in women's and men's crew and men's rugby affirm that athletic interests are widespread. This is also reflected in the intramurals, involving hundreds of students.

Fall Homecoming and the annual bonfire drew upon something primal in the student body. The labor to gather vast stacks of debris, mound it up, protect the fire from an early start by a rival college, and mount a rousing parade with automobiles and blaring horns through downtown Portland meant something in the 1950s. Then in 1964 the city invoked the "ten-by-ten square" ordinance on fires. Civic safety sounded the death knell to a cherished tradition. The *Log* lamented the passing event and suggested that within four years the Class of '68 would not only be thwarted in building a great fire but would fall victim to "a deep mass-psychological need to exert a sense of worth." Little did the *Log* writers know how assertive and socially active would be the class without a bonfire.

Homecoming has grown with the increasing numbers of alumni. The Alumni Association sponsors events under such themes as "Still Crazy After All These Years," "Old Enough to Know Better, Young Enough to Do It Again," and "Great Comebacks." In 1985 reunions of classes at five-year intervals commenced. Events have included the Athletic Hall of Fame induction, a football game with alumni band, lectures to stir memories, and award ceremonies.

Dormitory life is not like home. Having a brother or sister is one thing; living with forty women or fifty men is quite another. By the 1960s students were not satisfied with *in loco parentis* methods. The rule of house mothers, gender-disparate hours and regulations, and barriers to social interaction seemed inequitable in an era of rising social consciousness and cries for freedom. In 1963 the College established its first coeducational dorm, an experiment ahead of many major universities. Students articulated a system to justify the venture: group counseling, peer group control, and "self-discipline." Somehow Dean Hester Turner and President Howard accepted the proposal, but its implementation proved quite another matter. The structure of dormitory life seemed impervious to change.

In April 1966 women students heralded a breakthrough—no more sign-out cards to record when they left, where they were going, with whom they had gone, and when they were returning. The College even fixed new hours (for women only): 12:15 A.M. on school nights; 1:30 A.M. on weekends; and 2:00 A.M. for special events. Then came intervisitation. The dean of students accepted the daring idea to allow women to invite men to visit between 1:00 and 5:00 P.M. on Saturdays and Sundays. Students liked it, and advisers proposed that each dormitory floor be permitted to set its own intervisitation hours. President Howard deferred a decision in January and in April 1968 rejected the idea, arguing that residents of Copeland had "taken matters into their own hands" and other living units, as well, had failed to comply with the rules.

Tension over regulations brewed. In 1968 the Inter-Residence Hall Council upheld curfew rules because of alleged "infraction of the rules this year by a large majority of freshman women." Finally in November 1970 the College asked first-year women what they thought: 208 rejected any curfew; 2 voted in favor. Another year passed, however, before the double standard was removed and freshman women received the same freedom the men had.

Eating is one of the most difficult adjustments of student days. Whether it is SAGA, Marriott, Bon Appetit, the Rusty Nail or the Plattform, food purveyors seem unable to satisfy. Students press to move off campus; they yearn for that freedom. Then reality sets in: shopping, cooking, cleaning up. A few try paper plates, only to gain the disapproval of their ecologically-minded classmates. So a double standard develops. Students live off campus but buy-in or sneak-in to Fields. The resolution is never satisfactory, nor is the food ever good enough, but somehow most remain healthy. The 1978-79 yearbook commented: "People provided the atmosphere and flavor of SAGA even when the food didn't."

The College also has struggled with dress for meals. From 1942 to 1965 Sunday dinner meant Sunday clothes. When students challenged this, SAGA said "we did not make the rule." Dean Hester Turner confessed that the rule was "administration created." In 1966, 74.2 percent of dormitory residents opposed mandatory dress for Sunday dinner. Within a week administrative officers Howard, Hartzfeld-Jones, Turner, Gregg, Haldors, and Thayer capitulated. SAGA opened a casual dress line in Fields. Within a few Sundays nobody dressed up for gracious dining in Stamm.

Fall term rushes by: midterms, papers, and finals. The library—open twenty-four hours a day by the mid-1980s—hums with frantic activity: computers glow through the night; printers consume reams of paper; overloads and glitches feed anxiety. Students drink coffee, crash through notes, books, and articles, and try to bring under

control too much too long deferred. Until 1963 this rhythm shoved beyond Thanksgiving toward Christmas with traditional Hanging of the Green and the campus choir concert. A change in the College calendar ended campus observance of Christmas by students but set the stage in 1972 for the evolution of the Holiday Gala. Once sponsored by the president and now organized by the Alumni Association for alumni, friends, faculty, and staff, the Gala includes a president's reception in the Manor House, an alumni choir concert, and an evening of dancing to bands.

The campus becomes quieter in December. The staff labor on—the secretaries type winter term syllabi, bookstore clerks stock the shelves, administrators and faculty cope with performance reviews and tenure decisions, alumni office staff and volunteers decorate Templeton and the Manor for the Gala, and the development office solicits year-end gifts—but the pace slows. Some faculty and students set off on "Winterim" expeditions: "Hawaiian Insular Biology" or "Natural History of the Southwestern Deserts" (known as "Botany in Baja"). The curriculum committee voiced initial doubts but capitulated—and a lucky few study in the sun.

Winter is a time for remembering—the promise of life in spring, the vibrant growth of summer, the lazy warmth of fall. On Palatine Hill winter is a time for writing senior theses on international affairs, plunging into projects, rehearsing for plays and musical events, and trying new strategies to cope with mist and rain. It is not so much the volume of downpour as that it never seems to stop. Perhaps it is the gray sameness that provokes thinking about what was. "In memory," wrote Henry Thoreau, "is the more reality."

January is Oregon's cruelest month, offering mixed signals. It usually permits students to return to campus before it gets nasty. In 1944, 1963, and again in 1978 and 1979, icy blasts swept out of the Columbia Gorge. Freezing temperatures hit Pacific fronts, bringing moisture over the Coast Range. The campus was transformed into surreal fantasy. Then as freezing rain continued, trees snapped under the unaccustomed weight: limbs showered down, breaking electrical lines and plunging the campus into darkness. Lucky dormitory residents took a shower immediately and searched for off-campus friends with electricity. The unlucky settled in for cold days, picnic meals from SAGA, a moratorium on classes, and a yearning for warm water. In the best tradition of "the show must go on," Peter, Paul and Mary presented their 1963 ice storm concert to an appreciative student body.

Greek organizations played an important role in campus life. In 1953 there were seven fraternities and four sororities, incorporating 20 percent of the students. Two fraternities, Alpha Rho Omega and Sigma Alpha Sigma, and one sorority, Alpha Gamma, survived the move from Albany to Portland and the dislocations of World War II. All chapters were locals—chartered by the College and operated by its policies—that pursued social and service goals. They sponsored dances and campus-wide formals, decorated for Homecoming, Christmas, and May Fete, and reached out into the community. They took talent shows to local orphanages and hospitals, raised money to help homeless children, rallied blood donors, and sold greeting cards and "mums" to raise money.

The rapid growth of Greek organizations elicited considerable interest from national chapters, which repeatedly sought mergers.

▶ *Chris Abbruzzese, '93, enjoys a quiet moment in the sun at Albany Quadrangle, named for the predecessor of Lewis & Clark College.*

◄ Originally named the Women's Building, the Manor served as a women's dormitory in the 1940s. Erection of Akin Hall in 1949 expanded women's dormitory facilities. ▼ Since 1972, students enjoy rowing, sharing shells and a boathouse with the Station L Rowing Club. Coached by Charlie Brown, '85, 1989 National Champion in the Men's Open Quadruple Scull, rowing draws more than fifty dedicated athletes. Left to right are Gretchen Kloeppel, '92; Pam Jones, '92; Brenda Babeshoff, '91; Mikki Kistler, '92; Erica Balderson, '93; Hope McKee, '91; Didi Nelson, '93; Mira Morton, '92. Not pictured is Kathleen Peltier, '92, cox'n.

Those overtures seldom succeeded. Charles Charnquist, '58, later recalled: "Even in the early 1950s, Lewis & Clark fraternities and sororities stood strongly against any kind of discrimination. One year, the officers' cabinet of my fraternity, Kappa Phi Alpha, included a Japanese-American, an African-American, and a German Jew." The executive secretary of a national fraternity, Charnquist said, urged the officers to visit him at the Benson Hotel in Portland. But when he met them, he dropped all discussion of affiliation. Sigma Alpha Sigma, founded in 1938, finally agreed to a national affiliation but in 1962 withdrew. The campus chapter stated: "The members felt that the principles and policies of most national fraternities did not coincide with those of Sigma Alpha and were not in the best interest of Lewis and Clark College."

By the early 1970s Greek letter organizations had lost relevance. Sororities vanished as did fraternities except Sigma Alpha Epsilon and Sigma Phi Epsilon. The reputation for discrimination was one factor, but more important was the new social network emerging at the College. Easing of dormitory restrictions and development of intervisitation and coeducational living units contributed, but most important were the unique social ties and friendships generated through the overseas and off-campus study programs. The number of students involved far exceeded those once involved in fraternities and sororities. The shared experience of travel and study in other settings had profound and continuing effect on student life.

From the late 1940s into the early 1960s the campus mirrored a national era of growing prosperity. Few questioned hours of stuffing crepe paper into chicken wire, hanging balloons and streamers, painting murals on butcher paper, or transforming the commons or meeting rooms into settings for Mardi Gras, the Beatnik Ball, or a Pajama Dance. Crowds turned out for dances to celebrate Sadie Hawkins Day, Halloween, the Snow Ball Formal, and Sweethearts Ball. Then times altered, sharpened by causes of peace, war, social injustice, and student calls for action. New concerns and ways of expressing them came to campus. The Amicans, Erodelphians, Sacajaweans, and other groups—some surviving for decades—were gone, but others took their place. Among seventy-three organizations in 1990 were Adult Children of Alcoholics (ACOA), Alcoholics Anonymous, Amnesty International, Environmental Action Group, Fellowship of Christian Athletes, Forensics, Homophile, Martial Arts, National Abortion Rights Action League, Oregon Student Public Interest Research Group (OSPIRG), Reversals (a support group for dyslexics), Sailing Club, Students United for American Cultural Awareness, and the Whitewater Club.

The seasons of change involved important transitions in student life, almost always articulated and driven by student leaders. A turning point came in 1982 with the shift from a senate style of government in the ASLC to the emergence of student boards. For years student government used living groups as its representative basis. With the ebb and flow of students in off-campus and overseas programs and the number of upperclass students choosing to live in apartments, the basis of ASLC no longer seemed valid. Through winter and early spring student leaders, student affairs staff, and faculty explored models and focused on a structure related to the curriculum. The new government had an ASLC Student Council made up of members-at-large and the elected officers of boards: Budget and Finance, Policy Review, Information and Programs, Student Academic Affairs, and Student Communications. The Student Academic Affairs Board (SAAB) emerged as the fulcrum of activity; it drew representatives from each of the twenty-one majors

▲ The Lewis & Clark College rugby team battles PLU. Club sports—including rugby, lacrosse, crew, sailing, fencing, and skiing—compete against varsity teams from other colleges and universities.
► Several memorial gardens exist on campus. In 1990, the garden at the base of the Edna Holmes Terrace was dedicated to the memory of Vernon Long, professor of earth science, by the 1971 overseas study group to Australia and New Zealand, which he led.

▶ The annual Homecoming football game attracts fans of all ages, as alumni and future generations of Lewis & Clark students enjoy a fall weekend of activities. Ginny Buran Simich, '86, and her child join other young families in the Griswold stands. ▲ The Pioneers compete against Eastern Oregon at Griswold Stadium. Football fortunes at Lewis & Clark College ebb and flow. The early 1950s, mid-1960s, and early 1990s have produced conference champions.

The major college athletic directors
are being run by supporters, by alums
and donors. When that happens,
what's best educationally goes
out the window . . . Here, if we can't justify it
educationally, we don't have it.

FOOTBALL COACH FRED WILSON, 1965–85
Sports Illustrated, 1981

▲ Pioneer football fans enjoy their team at Griswold Stadium, named in honor of Graham Griswold, lumberman and trustee from 1952 to 1961. Griswold donated lumber and money for every building erected on the Fir Acres campus between 1944 and 1959.

and commenced 1982-83 with a budget of $49,080, two-thirds of the entire 1942 College budget in the first year at Fir Acres.

SAAB initiated a remarkable program. It tied to the faculty's Curriculum Committee through two voting student representatives. It initiated and funded a research program for students, extending projects beyond courses into self-designed, faculty-advised investigations. It inaugurated a Visiting Scholars Program, planned student assessment of the Society and Culture courses, and investigated the effectiveness of academic advising. Although sometimes criticized, SAAB was a student-run program directly related to the academic enterprise. It stimulated research, enriched teaching, and embodied the aspirations of generations of students who envisioned taking charge of their affairs while in college.

Winter days bring steady activity to Pamplin Sports Center. The men's and women's basketball teams practice and meet opponents for games, as do volleyball players and those engaged in swimming and diving competition. Hard practice sometimes pays off; in 1986 the women's volleyball team played in the NAIA national championship, losing to BYU Hawaii. The screech of tennis shoes against the gymnasium floor sounds from late afternoon into the evening. Students joust in fencing drills, throw each other in martial arts engagements, and dance in musical workouts.

Coaches Eldon Fix, Jim Goddard, and Dean Sempert presided over four decades of Pioneer basketball. Teams played off campus in rented facilities, in the old gym which burned in 1966, in Pamplin, and on the road. Sempert coached teams between 1963 and 1988, chalking up 356 victories to 309 losses. In 1981 he summed up the attitude of Lewis & Clark coaches when *Sports Illustrated* featured Dan Jones, '81, a three-sport letter winner. Sempert said of Jones:

> *I'm just glad to have as much of him as I do. I know the problems most coaches have in sharing a talent like that, even in high schools. But doesn't it go back to consistency? If we're hoping to teach students to be unselfish, to understand what's best for individuals, are we not obligated at least to try to be that way as well?*

Winter is also a time for enrichment activities. The ASLC Forum Series of the 1980s brought black activist Angela Davis, American Indian writer Vine DeLoria, Jr., geneticist Robert Sensheimer, and social and political critic Michael Harrington. The topics included "Toward a Just Society," "Combating Terrorism," "In Search of the Human," "The Energy Quandary," and "Ecology and the Human Future." The student-generated Intercultural Forum, a consortium with other colleges, brought new perspectives through minority speakers on a variety of issues. The State of the Art series in the 1980s offered performances by classical guitarists, pianists, string quartets, chamber groups, organists, puppet theatre, ballet, and thespians. These events spoke to the diversity in a lively college, a place of many opportunities.

Spring hints at the promise of summer with the sweet smell of cottonwoods, but backs away and turns gray and misty. Umbrellas, Goretex, wet socks, dripping trees, and slugs set the rhythm. There are also dogs—generations of them bearing familiar names—Jazzbo, Blackie, Rusty, Pasha, Peuce, and Bozo. Zephyr, who bunked in nearby Dunthorpe, catapulted to distinction in a nearly successful bid for ASLC president before dropping from favor. A "Dean of Dogs," the *Log* suggested during the debate over control of student

▲ Professor emeritus John Richards plays trumpet and directs the alumni band at the Homecoming football game. Alumni gather with students, faculty, and staff to enjoy Pioneer football and reminisce. The Homecoming/Reunion weekend program includes the alumni awards banquet, the all-class reunion dinner, the meeting of the national board of alumni, a presidential forum, class reunions, gatherings for overseas study programs, and a golf tournament.

animals, yet nothing happened. Springtime also brings visitors like Preacher Ray who, for a year or two, harangued students outside Templeton about the prospects of hell and damnation. Several rose to his bait and engaged in shouted exchanges as the preacher held his Bible high in his left hand and shook his right finger at vocal "sinners."

Spring has a sense of urgency. Seniors find the career center; juniors worry about declaring a major–something too long deferred; sophomores watch the postings on overseas and off-campus programs; and freshmen consider going home for summer with the realization that "home" may well be on Palatine Hill. Students renew vows to do better, plan ahead, and anticipate the impact of beautiful May days on unfinished papers and projects. Faculty cope with committee meetings and final advice to students regarding graduate schools. The grounds crew can barely keep up with the rush of new life: blackberry brambles, thriving lawns, insect-infested roses, and the onslaught of weeds.

March and April bring thematic conferences with speakers, panels, films, and discussions. Topical conferences draw on national and international figures for addresses and papers and can lead to sessions often running far into the night. May Fete vanished; the Sawdust Festival and the Renaissance Faire succeeded and also passed; but special symposia remain as enduring commitments of the College.

Students in theatre fine-tune their skills for more openings. The productions vary from year to year and decade to decade, but have included Greek tragedies, Renaissance drama, avant-garde plays, and both faculty- and student-directed performances. The plays of Euripedes, Strindberg, Chekhov, Williams, Ionesco, Beckett, and Pirandello have called for hours of rehearsal, work on costuming and set construction, and performances before audiences. Since 1972 when Professor Leon Pike led the first off-campus theatre program, students have had opportunity for encountering drama in New York City in courses alternating yearly with study in art. Construction of the new Fir Acres Theatre in 1976 ended the theatre-in-exile at Lake Oswego High School, which was leased following condemnation of the old facility by the fire marshal.

Since the first years of the Albany Collegiate Institute, students have participated in oratory contests. The process of research, organizing thoughts, producing sequential argument, and practicing in mock sessions is punctuated by high school and college tournaments and sending competitors to regional and national forensic events. Lewis & Clark students enter a variety of categories: impromptu, extemporaneous, debate, persuasive/oratory, and oral interpretation of literature. For several decades KLC has broadcast music and news to campus listeners and given hundreds of students a chance to work with broadcasting firsthand.

The rhythms of spring also bring to culmination frantic writing, layout, and production of yearbooks–appearing under a variety of names: *Voyageur*, *Convergence*, *Yiem Kimtah* on Palatine Hill and *ACTA*, *Takenah*, *Corsair* and the *Orange Peel* at Albany College. The *Pioneer Log* has chronicled student life, cultural events, faculty labors, and sporting news, continuing a tradition begun by Albany College's *Missive*, *The Echo*, and *The Student*. Alternative newspapers such as *Sacajawea's Voice*–an enduring, often irreverent offering–have also attracted student submissions and energies. The bound issues of the *Log*–black with gold on the spine and shelved in the Watzek Library–attest to decades of labor. May also yields special publications: essays on international affairs in

The Meridian, and final touches on poetry, short stories, photographs, and drawings, in campus literary magazines.

Spring sports begin in the mud–to the seeming delight of lacrosse and rugby players–and often end in more mud. The events of track and field, which have led the Pioneers to more than twenty district championships in the past fifty years, draw upon both team and individual competitors. The competition is on the field, though in the minds of many it is against the posted school records. Each year athletes nudge and, occasionally, topple a mark recorded on the panels in Pamplin's lobby. The baseball and softball teams play against opponents and the weather. Lewis & Clark teams have competed avidly in conference rounds, and in 1990 the baseball team participated in its first NAIA world series.

For seniors spring leads toward commencement events. The annual awards convocation with elections to Phi Kappa Phi, the Rena Ratte Award to the outstanding senior, and announcements of special fellowships and notices of honors begin the process. Then there are term papers, final exams, the off-campus senior party, arrival of family, departmental receptions, baccalaureate, and graduation. Smiles and tears, sunshine and shadow, accomplishment and uncertainty flood their lives. Almost before they know it, they are robing up, donning ribbons to signify countries of overseas study or legacy sashes to acknowledge prior family graduates, and walking in the procession beneath the firs, past the Manor House, before those who planned, prodded, encouraged, and hoped for this day. At the lead is the College mace: its symbolism speaking of the land where they have studied and the Indian civilizations which for thousands of years held sway in the Pacific Northwest. Then come the sounds of the orchestra, the shuffling of the audience, the focus of lights, and graduation. It is a bittersweet moment of relief, joy, and sadness. It is an ending and a beginning.

The rhythms of the life of the College are many: each event sets a different cadence; each life moves to a different tune; each experience generates a different memory and meaning. There is a legacy to all this, an enduring quality moving through time, touching the lives of people with aspirations. The success of the College in attaining its purpose is a measure of commitments: of students who understand the business of the life of the mind, of faculty who teach and become role models, of administrators and staff who serve and make the process work, and of friends who nurture and endow.

Lewis & Clark College has been blessed by those who have understood the value of helping the next generation. In her quiet way, Barbara Hirschi Neely, who died at age ninety-seven in 1990, affirmed that goal. Her participation in the College's deferred giving program through a series of trusts bequeathed more than six million dollars to endow scholarships. And others have given quietly but consistently to sustain the College in its efforts to meet budgets and cope with needs. Hall Templeton–avid oarsman, friend of the faculty, quiet counselor, and life trustee–is representative of those who have seen the College as an investment in the future.

Parents, grandparents, Presbyterians, Linn County farmers and business people, the Frank family, foundation boards, trustees, philanthropists, alumni, friends, staff, and faculty–all have nurtured the life of the mind and promoted high ambition. They have shared talents so the young could grow in mind, body, and spirit. Those who made the rhythms of the College possible have grasped the wisdom of the writer who said, "to every thing there is a season, and a time to every purpose under heaven."

Everyone here has a name,
and everyone has a face.
It's that kind of first-hand relationship
between professors and students,
which finally brings
all kinds of rewarding experience.

PROFESSOR JOHN K. RICHARDS
Journal of Lewis & Clark, 1975

▲ Sara Pozel, '92, shapes her pottery creation. Art students—majors and non-majors—work with faculty members who are nationally and internationally known artists. The Art Building houses a ceramics and sculpture studio; Peebles, the adjoining building, has studios for painting and drawing, graphic design, photography, and print-making, as well as a library of more than 30,000 art history slides.

▲ Mary Dimond, foreign student advisor, 1966-83, reminisces in 1991 with professor emerita and centenarian Emma Meier Schade, at a scholarship recognition luncheon. Professor Meier, known as "Frau Meier," taught German and Spanish at Albany College. A member of the first faculty at Lewis & Clark, she taught German and directed the choir. ► Oregon mist on the Manor House.

We sift from our habits
the nourishing ways:
listening, remembering, telling,
weaving a rooted companionship
with home ground.

KIM R. STAFFORD

Having Everything Right, 1987

▲ The annual Holiday Gala was initiated in 1972 as a "thank you" to a small group of donors. It contains elements of the traditional Hanging of the Green begun in 1946 and now draws as many as two thousand. It includes a chapel service and performance by the alumni choir, an open house hosted by the president in the Manor House, and dancing in Templeton College Center to music from different eras. ▶ Aaron Keaton, '93, performs with the College Choir, which, over the years, has traveled throughout the Western United States and Europe. In the 1950s and 1960s students sang in the College Choir, Chapel Choir, Madrigal Singers, and Men's Glee.

Snowflake designs lock;
they clasp in the sky,
hold their patterns one by one
down, spasms of loneliness,
each one God's answer.

PROFESSOR WILLIAM E. STAFFORD
"Walking the Wilderness," *Stories That Could Be True*, 1977

◄ Some winters bring tranquil moments to campus; others spawn arctic storms, which sweep through the Columbia Gorge and glaze everything with paralyzing ice. ▲ John Herlocker, '94, and Raven Winter, '94, conduct a physics experiment with a Bainbridge Tube.

▲ Unlike their Albany College predecessors, who danced by prescription, current Lewis & Clark students perform with acrobatic abandon. ▶ The original Campus Theatre was a World War II officers club, which was transplanted from Camp Adair. It provided space for convocations, commencement exercises, social activities, theatrical productions, and offices for the music and drama departments. The Fir Acres Theatre, opened in 1977, includes a 250-seat main stage performance/teaching theatre, a Black Box experimental teaching theatre, a scene shop, a costume room, and a design lab.

Students come with very high ambitions
for themselves — in a sense,
being ready to extend themselves,
being ready to work as hard as it takes
to do what they are doing.

PROFESSOR STEPHANIE ARNOLD
Theatre Department alumni newsletter, 1988

▼ Built in 1965 and renovated in 1990, the original Council Chamber was modelled after the United Nations Assembly Hall. Professor Karlin Capper-Johnson advised the Model United Nations and started the International Affairs Symposium, a tradition which continues with rotating student leadership under Professor Joe Ha.
► The Winged Ox stands at the entrance of Agnes Flanagan Chapel. A symbol of sacrifice, it is ascribed to Luke, who wrote of the sacrificial death of Christ. Carved by Lelooska, the original cedar sculpture is displayed in the Aubrey R. Watzek Library.

◄ The grounds around the Manor House have witnessed repeated student protests: the war in Vietnam, divestment of the College endowment portfolio, and the war in the Persian Gulf. ▲ Darcy Lyon, '93, shown with a peace symbol, echoed an earlier era, as did the peace tent erected during the Persian Gulf War in 1991.

▲ Jasmine Wibisono, '93, Indonesia. ▶ The original Fir Acres estate grounds included a rock garden and extensive floral plantings south of the glass dome conservatory. The dome was destroyed in 1962 during the Columbus Day Storm. The plantings have been replaced with sculpture gardens which provide an idyllic setting for the display of work by Bruce West, '61, lecturer in art.

Our aim is not to show the student
what to think — but how to think.

PROFESSOR JOHN HARRINGTON, 1963

◄ In the 1920s, the City of Portland began paving downtown streets. The original cobblestone was secured by architect Herman Brookman and used throughout the estate. ▲ In 1991, the Alumni Association named the Alumni Citation in recognition of Professor Donald Balmer's forty years of teaching and his support of Lewis & Clark College graduates. Shannon Ratliff, '91, Margette Baptist, '91, and Tim Bailey, '91, participate in a political science seminar.

*Our concern for creativity
parallels our concern for the individual.*

PROFESSOR PHYLLIS YES, 1983

▲ Student petitions and demonstrations in the 1960s for longer library hours met with frustration; by the 1980s, however, Watzek Library operated twenty-four hours each weekday of the school year. ▶ James Meakin, '91, completes a colorful sculpture under the direction of Professor Ken Shores. Each year seniors mount an exhibit of their artistic creations in Templeton College Center.

I will leave Lewis and Clark
with a completed degree
but definitely not
with a completed education.
I feel that I am just starting.

ROMALIA K. STICKNEY, '83
Yiem Kimtah, 1983

◄ Shawna Meyer, '94, women's softball pitcher; background, Kris Rider, '93. The Joe Huston Fields are used for baseball, softball, and soccer practice. ▲ The campus retains original plantings of rhododendrons and azaleas selected by Herman Brookman and Fir Acres gardeners. Special gifts have led to new plantings.

The landscape brings me thoughts of human
strengths and their personal manifestations
of "soul." Houses of years, of centuries,
embued themselves into the land
as self-created monuments to that soul. Red tile
roofs of Spain are the history. Tilled plots of land
are the economics. The politics are life . . .

MEGAN VORHEES, '93
Journal entries, Ecuador overseas study program, 1990
"Insider's Guide '91"

▲ Rebecca Booth, '94, and Kolin Kothmann, '92, study on the
Manor terrace. Named for Edna Frank Holmes, the Manor terrace
was the site of numerous cultural events in the 1920s and 1930s,
including concerts of the Portland Junior Symphony. ▶ "Deferred
maintenance" at Albany Quadrangle creates a beauty of its own.

◄ Biology professor Edwin Florance continues a tradition started by Benjamin Thaxter, using the campus natural habitat for instruction. ▲ Tim Gaillard, '91, varsity tennis standout, plays on the Pamplin courts. Robb Tanaka, '94, practices at Joe Huston Field. In 1990, the baseball team, coached by Jerry Gatto, played in the NAIA World Series. Opportunities for women in team sports increased during the 1970s and 1980s. Besides varsity basketball, softball, soccer, swimming, diving, tennis, track, cross country, and volleyball, the College added fencing, lacrosse, crew, and skiing clubs.

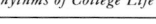

▶ Outdoor activities found organized expression over the years in such groups as Trodse, Trekenspielers, Alpine Club, and Ski Club. Since 1978, trips sponsored by the College Outdoors program have become a centerpiece of student activities. ▲ The outdoor swimming pool, built with the original estate in the 1920s, is used primarily during the summer months, when it becomes a haven for students, alumni, and College neighbors. It is complemented by Zehnbauer Swim Pavilion, an indoor facility with a 25 yard, 8 lane competition pool with one and three meter diving boards.

It's one thing to be self-absorbed
and quite another to be self-aware.
It comes down to a matter of being open,
of seeing, of recognizing the smallest change
in yourself and others as being of value,
of remaining intrigued enough by life
to welcome its constant renewal.

CARTOONIST GARRY TRUDEAU
Commencement Address, 1979

▶ Refurbished in 1991 through the "Just Fix It" campaign of track alumni, corporate and foundation support, trustees and friends, the Eldon Fix Track, Fisher Field, and Griswold Stadium serve competitions in track and field, football, and soccer. Pictured left to right, Eric Olson, '91; Jeff Miller, '93; and Glen Ferguson, '94, sprint around the track. ▲ In the 1950s, the dovecote atop the gardeners workroom on the original estate was the focus of spirited rivalry between "pro-squirrel" and "pro-pigeon" factions of the faculty.

Like the trees, we are visitors, guests of earth.

KIM R. STAFFORD
Entering the Grove, 1990

◄ Flowering cherry tree in storm near Templeton College Center.
▲ William E. Stafford, professor emeritus and poet laureate of Oregon, 1974-90, taught at Lewis & Clark College for three decades. Stafford's creative energies have inspired generations of students and have attracted a national audience. His son, Kim R. Stafford, is director of the College's Northwest Writing Institute.

. . . I've gained vast amounts of knowledge, filled
my heart with unforgettable memories and made
friends so dear that it must be fate. . . .
What do you say to someone you've just spent some
of the best years of your life with?
Goodbye, good luck, make me proud, I love you.

CLAUDIA JOHNSON, '85
Yiem Kimtah, 1985

▲ The tradition of academic dress began several centuries ago in universities where cap, gown, and hood were needed for warmth. Subsequently this has become a ceremonial costume with certain standardized features. The hood is lined with the official college colors of the degree-conferring institution. *Above right:* Zuigaku Kodachi, lecturer in Japanese, reviews the commencement program prior to ceremonies. ► The 1991 commencement ceremony for the College of Arts and Sciences, held in Pamplin Sports Center.

Appropriately educated, a graduate
of Lewis & Clark will emerge with a keener sense
of the present and a more active curiosity,
with an informed respect for the environment
and a genuine engagement with other cultures.
Such are the habits of the heart
that make up the character of this College.

PRESIDENT MICHAEL MOONEY
Inaugural address, 1990

◄ Michael Mooney, president, looks with pride on the graduating class. ▲ The Lewis & Clark diploma formally certifies that a student has satisfactorily completed the requirements for a specific degree. It symbolizes years of hard work, sacrifice, determination, courage, growth, and achievement. It is cause for celebration.

ACKNOWLEDGMENTS

The genesis of this book and its nurturing stemmed from the inspiration of Michael Ford, alumni director, and Michael Mooney, College president. Ford articulated the vision, organized and coordinated the effort, co-authored the captions, and marketed the book. Mooney backed the project. To them I am most appreciative, for they had the trust to proceed with this task and provided the inspiration and encouragement to bring it to completion. My thanks also to the Board of Alumni for its sponsorship and support.

Many contributed to this project—current staff, retired faculty and administrative officers, alumni, and friends. To those who shared insights, recounted stories, assisted in photo identifications, and guided accuracy, I am grateful. Martha Montague's *Lewis and Clark College, 1867-1967* proved a storehouse of information about the details of the institution's development. The archives, nurtured by Lecturer Emeritus James Holton, contained more than I wanted to know. Douglas Erickson, the current archivist, cheerfully searched for files, publications, photographs, and materials. Dorothy Sherman and Margery Crist recalled their childhood days at Fir Acres, and John and Ruth Howard graciously reminisced about their twenty-one years at the College.

To John Howard and John Brown who brought me to Lewis & Clark; to thousands of students with whom I have had opportunity to teach, study, and travel; to colleagues who patiently answered questions; to my wife, Patti, and children who have seen too little of me during this undertaking; and to my parents, Dow and Anna Beckham, who taught me to love learning, I am most appreciative.

Stephen Dow Beckham
Professor of History

Special acknowledgment is made to the following:

Alumni Advisory Committee:

Professor Emeritus John Anderson
Nancy Budrow, '71
Tod Burton, '81
Charles Charnquist, '58
Janet Eastman, '49
Peter Edwards, '88
Homer Groening
Brenden Hyde, '87
Dewey Kelly, '74
Karl Klooster, '62
Derek Larson, '90
Susan Sharp, '72, '75, '81
Nona Shearer, '74
William Shearer, '31
Timothy Swain, '63
Jack Venables, '56
Peter Vlahos, '57
Kelly Krein Weber, '86

Editorial Advisory Committee:

John Callahan
Michael Ford
Judy McNally
Michael Mooney
Mary Anne Normandin

Board of Alumni presidents:

Wendy Bond, '77, '79
Maggie Koenig Englund, '79
David Taylor, '74

College and Alumni Relations staff:

Janie Attridge
Carolyn Bowden
Martha Crary Gregory
Mary Potter

Alumni Responding to Requests:

Tony Abena '86
L. Annette Adcock, '29
Cathy Huntley Bernhard, '67, '85
Bob Bissell, '54
Meredith Norton Davis, '78
Judy Fine-Eichner, '78
Michael T. Fritz, '72
David R. Grube, '79
David H. Lee, '50
Sandy Osborne, '72
Cynthia Owens, '80
John Pearce, '90
Alan R. Pence, '71
Robert Potts, '35
Kylene Johnson Quinn, '77
Terry Supahan, '81
Leon Vitovitch, '80

Student Researchers:

Prassi de Mel, '93
Laura Hollingshead, '91
John Marshall, '92
Kristin Winnie, '91

Graphic Arts Center Publishing Company

Jean Andrews
Ross Eberman
Charles M. Hopkins
Richard Owsiany
Douglas Pfeiffer
Julie Pitz
Mary Ross
Ken Rowe
Mark Weber

▲ Graduates who have alumni relatives are identified at commencement with an orange legacy sash embroidered in black with the graduate years of other family members from Lewis & Clark and Albany. Pictured above with his parents, Jay Bress, '91, joins his brother Rob, '86, as a member of the Alumni Association.

CHRONOLOGY

1867   Founders' Day, February 2. The Oregon legislature granted a charter to Albany Collegiate Institute. William Monteith presided as first president with forty students enrolled.

1873   Four women students–College's first alumnae–graduated.

1884   Richard Hopwood Thornton began teaching the first law students in Northwestern College of Law.

1885   President Elbert Condit discovered a deficit of $894 and described the College finances as "desperate."

1886   Northwestern College of Law graduated first two students to begin practicing law.

1891   Albany students selected black and orange as school colors to honor Condit's alma mater, Princeton. Corvallis College, later O.S.U., chose the same colors several years later.

1892   Albany's first school song, "The Orange and the Black," was adopted.

1902   The *ACTA* appeared as the first yearbook. Many name changes followed: *Takenah* (1911), *The Orange Peal* (1916), *Corsair* (1930), *Voyageur* (1943), and *Yiem Kimtah* (1982). Between 1970 and 1977 nobody produced a yearbook; this period is remembered as the Dark Ages of the College.

1905   The ACI became officially Albany College.

1915   The University of Oregon *thought* it moved the law school to Eugene. Northwestern College of Law–with faculty, students, and library–remained in Portland.

1924   Lloyd and Edna Frank and children moved to Fir Acres.

1930   *Song Lore of Albany College* was published and dedicated to former President Wallace Howe Lee.

1935   The football team gained national notoriety with record of 28 successive losses over a four-year period.

1938   Albany campus closed with June graduation; the surviving students and faculty moved to Portland.

1942   Trustees named Morgan Odell president and on June 30 purchased Fir Acres for $46,000. The name Lewis & Clark College was adopted, and classes started with 135 students and 8 faculty. The *Pioneer Log* began publication.

1943   Victor Creed, trustee, led efforts to restore rose gardens and plant some seventeen hundred bushes under care of the Men's Garden Club. The students raised rhubarb and vegetables.

1946   Enrollment mounted with the returning veterans, and the College began importing military buildings to become new classrooms, offices, a theatre, and dining commons. The students adopted the name "Pioneers."

1949   The basketball team under coach Eldon Fix won the College's first Northwest Conference title.

1950   Coach Joe Huston's football team defeated San Francisco State, 61-7, in the Pear Bowl in Medford.

1954   Graham Griswold was honored with the dedication of the stadium; Platt Hall was named for trustee Clemmer Platt.

1957   Capitol Records produced an album of the College Choir directed by Stanley Glarum.

1960   The trustees named John R. Howard College president. John F. Kennedy visited the campus in his campaign for president of the United States.

1962   The speech of Gus Hall, American communist, tested free inquiry; Hall proved boring but free inquiry won. Students found first trip to NAIA national basketball tournament and Columbus Day storm more interesting (as did trustees).

1963   The College adopted the 3-3 program with three terms of eleven weeks, and students began Otto Sack Day to honor the dedicated but overworked gardener, Otto Sack.

1964   Lecture series began, honoring the late Dr. Arthur Throckmorton of the History Department. Students found Japanese baths in Forest dorms.

1965   The Northwestern College of Law merged with Lewis & Clark College.

1966   The gymnasium burned providing an opportunity for an indoor swimming pool and Pamplin Sports Center. College severed ties with Presbyterian Church.

1967   Professor Martha Montague authored a history of the College to honor its first hundred years. Crews completed the Watzek Library and Agnes Flanagan Chapel.

1970   The *Environmental Law Review* commenced publication; law students moved into new facilities on the campus.

1972   Undergraduates occupied the Manor to protest renewed bombing in Southeast Asia.

1973   Lewis & Clark dropped religion course requirements.

1974   Professor William Stafford named Oregon's Poet Laureate.

1977   Fir Acres Theatre opened with "The Cherry Orchard" by Anton Chekhov, Russian playwright.

1978   The College Outdoors Program began; Pioneer Athletic Hall of Fame inducted ten charter members.

1979   Ice storm closed the Fir Acres campus for five days.

1980   Mount St. Helens erupted during the Renaissance Faire.

1981   James Gardner inaugurated as president. *Sports Illustrated* featured Dan Jones, '82, as a three-sport athlete.

1982   ASLC reorganizes; Senate disbanded. New governance model included Student Academic Affairs Board (SAAB).

1985   Basic Inquiry (BI) replaced Society and Culture program as a General Education requirement.

1987   *Rolling Stone* named Lewis & Clark a "cool school." Trustees agreed to "divest" investments in South Africa.

1988   Liz Walker Downing, '81, won Women's World Biathlon.

1990   President Michael Mooney announced the scholarship endowment of Barbara Hirschi Neely of $6.1 million and endowed professorships honoring Dr. Robert Pamplin, Jr., '64, William Swindells, Sr., and Morgan Odell.

1991   *U.S. News and World Report* named the Environmental Law program second in the United States. The College completed a new campus master plan.

1992   College celebrated 125th anniversary of founding as Albany Collegiate Institute; 50th anniversary of move to Fir Acres campus and name change to Lewis & Clark College; 30th anniversary of overseas programs.

BIBLIOGRAPHY

The College Archives hold extensive collections of presidential papers, faculty minutes, records of the deliberations of the Board of Trustees, ephemera (playbills, posters), photographs, audio recordings, reports of special commissions and committees, and memorabilia. In addition to these materials, the essays and captions for the illustrations have drawn on the following:

Abbott, Bruce A. and Phyllis Stagias
    1974   The Groundwork. Calligraphed Album, Lewis and Clark College, Portland, Oregon.

The Advocate

Albany College Bulletin

Annual Catalogue of Albany College

Anonymous
    1903   "Thomas Monteith," *Portrait and Biographical Record of Willamette Valley Oregon*. Chapman Publishing Co., Chicago, Illinois.

    1929   Silhouettes: 'Architecture is a Man's Art, Immense, Historical . . .' *Spectator*, 45(12) [May 4]:7.

    1932   Glorious Gardens on the Estate of Lloyd Frank, Esq., at Portland, Oregon. *Country Life*, 60(6):62-63.

    1942   Albany College Moves to New Home, *The Spectator* (Portland, Oregon), August.

            Albany College Diamond Jubilee Brings New President; New Campus, *The Voice of American Women*, September.

            College Gains Campus Site, *Oregonian* (Portland, Oregon), July 1.

Annual Catalogue of Albany College, 1878-1942

Brookman, Herman
    1925   Photo Album presented to Lloyd and Edna (Levy) Frank. Dorothy (Frank) Sherman, Portland, Oregon.

Elwyn, Reed and Jonathon Horn
    1978   National Register Nomination, M. Lloyd Frank Estate. MS, State Historic Preservation Office, Salem, Oregon.

Environmental Law Review

Harris, Leon
    1977   *Merchant Princes: An Intimate History of Jewish Families Who Built Great Department Stores*. Harper & Row, Publishers, New York.

Heltzel, Ellen Emry
    1982   An Era of Gracious Living. *Oregonian* (Portland, Oregon), August 26.

Hitchcock, Henry-Russell
    1958   *Architecture Nineteenth and Twentieth Centuries*. Penguin Books, Baltimore, Maryland.

Holmes, Edna
    n.d.   Scrapbook. Dorothy (Frank) Sherman, Portland, Oregon.

    1973   Interview with Bruce Abbott. MS typescript. Lewis and Clark College Archives, Portland, Oregon.

The Journal of Lewis and Clark College

Lewis and Clark College Bulletin

Lewis and Clark College Catalog

Lowenstin, Steven
    1987   *The Jews of Oregon, 1850-1950*. Jewish Historical Society of Oregon, Portland, Oregon.

Montague, Martha Frances
    1967   *Lewis and Clark College, 1867-1967*. Binfords & Mort, Publishers, Portland, Oregon.

Moore, Kenny
    1981   The Three-Sport Man: Hail and Farewell, *Sports Illustrated* 54(20), May 11:66-80.

Moxness, Ron
    1944   City's Cinderella Campus Due for Postwar Build-up, *Oregonian* (Portland, Oregon), December 3.

Mullen, Floyd C.
    1971   *The Land of Linn: An Historical Account of Linn County, Oregon*. Dalton's Printing, Lebanon, Oregon.

Mumford, Lewis
    1972   *Roots of Contemporary American Architecture*. Dover Publications, Inc., New York.

Nokes, Richard
    1942   After 75 Years of Struggle, Fortune Seems to Have Smiled on Presbyterian Institution, *Oregonian* (Portland, Oregon), September 13.

Odell, Morgan S.
    1942   Letter of June 22 [to visitors at Fir Acres], College Archives.

Orange Peal

Pintarich, Paul
    1974   Herman Brookman: Masterworks Remain. *Oregonian* (Portland, Oregon), January 6.

Pioneer Log

Platt, C. W.
    1941   Letter of July 25 to Mrs. Ralph H. Mort, Women's Albany College League, College Archives.

Potts, Robert
    n.d.   Albany College Memorabilia Collection, Albany, Oregon.

Takenah

Thompson, Lindsay Taylor
    1984   The Founder: Richard Hopwood Thornton, 1846-1925. *The Advocate*, pp. 23-28.

Van Cleve, Jane
    1976   Brookman Designed With Passion. *Willamette Week* (Portland, Oregon), April 19.

Vaughan, Thomas and Virginia Guest Ferriday, eds.
    1974   *Space, Style, and Structure*. 2 volumes. Oregon Historical Society, Portland, Oregon.

Voyageur

Williams, Edgar
    1978   *Illustrated Historical Atlas Map of Marion and Linn Counties, Oregon*. Edgar Williams & Co., San Francisco, California.

Yiem Kimtah